FOR
WOMEN

A 365-DAY DEVOTIONAL

BroadStreet
PUBLISHING

BroadStreet Publishing
Savage, Minnesota, USA

A DAILY WORD FOR WOMEN

978-1-4245-6376-0 (faux)
978-1-4245-6377-7 (e-book)

Devotional entries composed by Rachel Flores and Suzanne Niles.

Design by Chris Garborg | garborgdesign.com
Editorial services by Sarah Eral and Michelle Winger | literallyprecise.com

Printed in China.

21 22 23 24 25 26 27 7 6 5 4 3 2 1

The unfolding of
your words gives light;
it gives understanding
to the simple.

Psalm 119:130 NIV

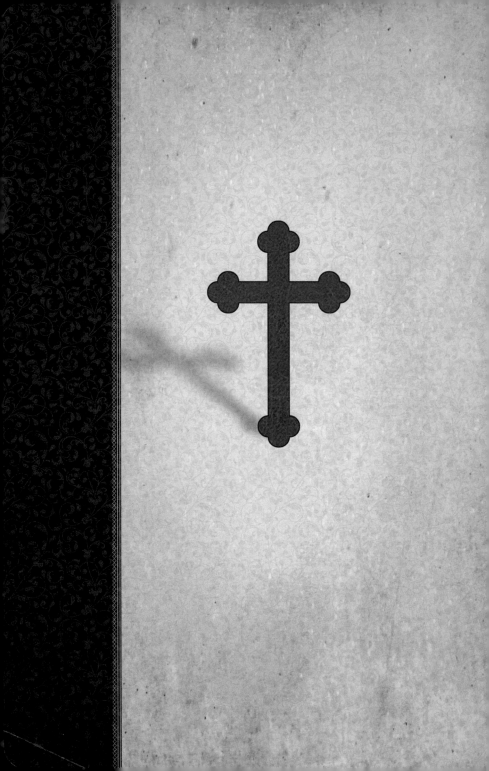

Introduction

Our daily routines sometimes condition us into comfortable living. We settle for repeated rhythms and expect our lives to change. Day after day, month after month, year after year, we find happiness in things that satisfy only our immediate needs and desires. Our hearts long for more, but we settle for less.

Time spent in God's presence empowers you to be a woman of grace, strength, and compassion. This devotional presents a motivating word for you to reflect on each day. Allow this daily word to inspire you as you prayerfully consider the Scripture, devotion, and thought-provoking question built around it.

Let Jesus disrupt your daily pattern of living and give you eyes to see the alternative life he offers. A life that satisfies beyond your temporary needs and desires. A life that brings light to your heart and home. A life that spills over into the people around you. A life that generates more life.

January

✝

God is our refuge and strength,
Always ready to help in times of trouble.

Psalm 46:1 nlt

Purposeful

In their hearts humans plan their course,
But the LORD establishes their steps.

PROVERBS 16:9 NIV

With the flip of your day planner page, you can feel it in the air. There is a buzz about the first day of January that moves so many of us to plan. Looking at the blank paper laid before us, we can't help but get excited at the possibility of new and better things to come in the year. Hope rises as we scribble down each resolution or goal. As women of God, we have specific goals to write down. To live impactful lives, we must submit our plans to God.

First, pray throughout your life, and listen closely to what God might want you to add or to cut out. Listen for relationships that need tending, for forgiveness that needs to be given. God is in the day-to-day just as much as he is in the big moments. Next, instead of focusing only on your goals this year, find a characteristic of God you want to learn more about. Do you want to see his mercy splashed across the pages of this year? Do you want to notice his goodness working all around you? Make an attribute of God a priority for your year along with your goals, and the direction of your year will be God's way for your life.

How can you join with what God is doing in your life?

Decisive

When you ask, you must believe and not doubt,
because the one who doubts is like a wave of the sea,
blown and tossed by the wind.

JAMES 1:6 NIV

We live in the information age. At our fingertips, we have more research, opinions, and knowledge than previous generations could have dreamed of. Though this can be to our advantage, it can also be our downfall. Too much information can create indecisiveness inside of us, paralyzing us. To be decisive women of God, we must be firmly planted in his Word.

The Bible is truth, and what it says should be the final say in our lives. We must continue to turn to God's Word daily, familiarizing ourselves with the truth. When we do this, we become anchored in truth, and our ability to make wise and good decisions increases. We will know about the character of God, and we will know what to ask for. We will learn to trust God when he sets our feet on a certain path. Keep his Word at the front of your mind, and you will be able to confidently face all that life has to offer.

What decisions do you need to invite God into today?

Composed

I have calmed and quieted my soul,
like a weaned child with its mother,
like a weaned child is my soul within me.
PSALM 131:2 ESV

What does it mean to be composed? For ages, the church has been telling women to act a specific way, and some claim that to be godly means to be quiet. Is this what it means for us to be composed? What do you do when you find yourself bursting with a message? What about when you laugh a little too loudly with joy? If you are supposed to be calm, why does it feel like God created you to be the opposite?

Sister, take heart. A calm soul does not always mean a quiet personality. A shy manner is not the key to rest your soul in Christ. God has given you specific gifts and abilities; he has made you to reach people in specific ways. Listen to his voice when deciding when to speak and when to remain quiet. Your soul can be undisturbed by the things of this world because it is a soul rooted in Christ's love. Shake off the stereotypes and shame that might hinder you from using the gifts God has given you. A composed woman is not measured by the volume of her voice, but by the source of the serenity of her spirit, and Jesus is our source.

How can you discern between cultural ideas and the truth of Scripture?

Bold

> *"Don't be afraid, for I am with you.*
> *Don't be discouraged, for I am your God.*
> *I will strengthen you and help you.*
> *I will hold you up with my victorious right hand."*
>
> ISAIAH 41:10 NLT

If you had no fear, nothing holding you back, what would you do? What would you believe without doubt? What move would you make? There is no time like the present to make bold moves for God. A few days ago, we wrote down our resolutions, our goals, and our dreams. Look at that list again. What could God be asking you to step out into right now? Where could God be nudging you to dream a little bigger?

There is no mountain, no dream, and no obstacle too big for our God. He is the one who empowers us, freeing us from shame and fear, so that we can lives that are bold for his glory. Though it is God who brings the freedom, the victory, and the power, we still have to take the steps. It might be something as small as knocking on your neighbor's door or something as large as moving to a new home. God is not limited by our circumstances. He wants to move in your life. Take some time in prayer to ask God how he wants you to be bold today.

How can you be bold today?

Abiding

"Abide in Me, and I in you.
As the branch cannot bear fruit itself,
unless it abides in the vine,
neither can you, unless you abide in Me."

JOHN 15:4 NKJV

Abide is possibly one of the most important words in the Bible. It is essential to the believer's life to learn how to abide in Christ. To abide means to dwell. Think of your home. What's the difference between a house and a home? A house is just a structure. You feel comfortable and safe in a home. It's the place you can most be yourself and let your guard down.

God did not send his Son to create distance between him and humanity. He sent his Son to dwell with us, be close to us, and draw us closer to himself. God wants you to be at your most vulnerable and open in his presence. We are trained well in the art of superficial relationships. It is now time, through study of the Word and prayer, to learn how to have a deep relationship with Jesus. He is trustworthy and kind. Abiding in Christ will lead to obedience to his Word, and it will also lead to fruit for his glory. Jesus is calling you to come home today, to dwell with him and learn from him. Won't you answer his call?

How do you abide in Jesus?

Appropriate

*In those days Israel had no king;
everyone did as they saw fit.*

JUDGES 21:25 NIV

This short phrase from the book of Judges speaks volumes about the state of the culture of God's chosen people during that time. The standard for what was deemed good was reduced to whatever a person felt was appropriate for them. Driven by their sinful natures, some of the more horrific stories in the Bible follow in the book of Judges. A people left to their own devices will bend toward their sinful nature, twisting and mutilating truth until it is unrecognizable.

With our current culture screaming for everyone to follow their own truth, the familiarity to the Judges passage is eerie. As women of God, we know better. We have the solid, unshakeable, unchanging Word of God to root our lives. The Word of God tells us what is appropriate for life and what is not. We must adopt his standard as our own standard for truth if we desire to live a life that glorifies Christ. Examine yourself today. In what ways are you adopting the attitude and lifestyle of what is right in your eyes, instead of humbly asking God what is right in his eyes?

What opinions of the world have you adopted? Do they align with God's Word?

Assured

Being fully assured that what God had promised,
He was able also to perform.

ROMANS 4:21 NASB

Two little girls were arguing in the backseat of a car. One claimed that no one can know what happens to you after you die. The other one, wise for her seven years and having recently come to an understanding of the gospel, proclaimed, "Yes I can! I'm going to heaven, and I know that because my daddy told me it's true." The beauty in this little girl's statement is multifaceted, but what stands out most is her confidence in the truth her daddy had told her. She had complete, assured faith that what her father had said was true.

The Bible is full of the Father's promises to us. Promises for eternal life, rewards, peace, his presence—the wonderful list goes on and on. Let us be like that little girl, full of confidence in what our heavenly Father has promised us. Let us tell others about these promises, knowing that God always keeps his word. No lie is found in him. What peace can come from this great assurance!

How can you remember God's promises today?

Character

We rejoice in our sufferings, knowing that suffering
produces endurance, and endurance produces character,
and character produces hope.

ROMANS 5:3-4 ESV

Scan the headlines and you will find it: another pastor or spiritual leader caught up in a sinful scandal. It's heartbreaking and discouraging but no longer shocking to us. It does bring up questions within us, one of which is probably, "How can this be avoided?" Dear sister, you are a spiritual leader in whatever capacity you serve in now. At work, at church, as a mother, as a friend—leadership has many faces.

The most important part of maintaining integrity as a leader is the character development you do when no one is watching. The deeper life, the internal life, matters far more than the exterior. Are you daily in God's Word? Are you in communion with him through prayer? Do you have people around you that you can confess your sins to and who lovingly call out sin in your life? Think of it like an iceberg. The top of the iceberg, the part we see, is probably ten percent. The strength and mass of the iceberg lies in the ninety percent we don't see, the part below the surface. That's your character. What is making up your ninety percent?

How can you grow in character and produce change?

Captivating

"Whoever drinks of the water that I shall give him will never thirst. But the water that I shall give him will become in him a fountain of water springing up into everlasting life."

JOHN 4:14 NKJV

Go ahead and read all of John chapter 4. It's a story most are familiar with. The story of the woman at the well is a look at a woman who becomes captivated by Jesus. When we encounter Jesus, we cannot help but be changed. As your life in Christ grows through time in his presence, Christ becomes more and more precious to you. Through experience, you start to understand why the disciples left everything to follow him. You understand why, when Jesus asked them if they would turn away from him, they declared, "Where else can we go?"

You can also understand the woman at the well, who was so struck by his presence that she declared it to the entire town that had shunned her. A life captivated by Christ is a transformed, bright, shining life. Examine your own life. Does Jesus captivate your soul, or do you find other things sitting on the throne? Make sure Jesus is on the throne of your heart today. Let him consume your passion.

How can you keep your eyes from wandering and your heart from straying?

Authoritative

All Scripture is inspired by God and is useful for teaching, for showing people what is wrong in their lives, for correcting faults, and for teaching how to live right.

2 TIMOTHY 3:16 NCV

In many northern parts of our world, little villages spring up on lakes and rivers in January. Tiny houses cluster on the frozen water, inhabited by ice fishers. You can even see people driving their vehicles across miles of water that has become ice. Many checks and tests have been done by fishermen and local officials to make sure the ice is reliable enough to hold the weight of vehicles and trailers. The fishermen display quite a bit of trust in the DNR's authority and other sources as they roll onto the icy tundra.

In the same way, the Bible is our authoritative source that we cast all our weight upon. It will never break out from under you; it is never unreliable. The Bible is the Word of God given to us, and it has so many wonderful uses in our lives. No matter what you are looking for, make sure the authoritative standard for truth in your life and worldview is the Bible.

How can you build your life on God's Word, knowing it will never fail you?

Empathetic

We do not have a high priest who is unable to sympathize with our weaknesses, but one who in every respect has been tempted as we are, yet without sin.

HEBREWS 4:15 ESV

To be known is one of the deepest desires of the human heart. However, we humans go to great lengths to protect our true selves from the pain that can occur from being exposed and left unloved or abandoned. Even in our most intimate relationships, we try to hide away, afraid of the repercussions that would come if they truly knew us.

The beauty of our relationship with Christ is that he knows. He knows all about all the parts of you that you hide away, the parts that you think are going to make him not love you. He not only knows your deepest weaknesses, but he has felt them. He's not looking down on you, shaking his head in disgust at your weakness. He's also not warily patting you on the back, full of pity and wondering how you could be this way. He is empathic toward you and your weakness. He gets it. He came to earth, fully man and fully God, so he could fully empathize with us.

How can you draw near to Jesus today?

Empowered

*"You will receive power
when the Holy Spirit comes on you."*

ACTS 1:8 NIV

Even though Jesus came back and taught the disciples after his resurrection, the great commission he gave them before his final ascent must have felt like a daunting task. This is evident to us as we find them at the beginning of the book of Acts, huddled at home, afraid. Jesus told them to take the gospel to the whole world. What an overwhelming command!

You will face many things in your life that will be overwhelming. Maybe some are the big dreams you wrote down at the beginning of the year, or recent news that came out of left field. Whatever your situation, the same truth that was available to the disciples is available to you. You have been given authority, strength, and confidence to face whatever it is by the power of the Holy Spirit. The Holy Spirit is God. He is not a lesser being or a poor substitute teacher. You have the spirit of the living God living inside of you. The same power that raised Christ from the dead is what you are empowered with today.

How do you feel empowered when you are overwhelmed?

Doubtless

"Why are you frightened?" he asked. "Why are your hearts filled with doubt? Look at my hands. Look at my feet. You can see that it's really me. Touch me and make sure that I am not a ghost, because ghosts don't have bodies, as you see that I do." As he spoke, he showed them his hands and his feet.

LUKE 24:38-40 NLT

Contrary to popular belief, it is not a sin to doubt. Certainly, doubt can be a vehicle that drives us to ungodly ends but doubt in and of itself is not a sin. We should allow our doubts to drive us into the arms of our Savior. There is no question, hesitation, or doubt you may have that is too big for him. He welcomes you and your questions with open arms.

In our Scripture today, Jesus knew exactly what Thomas needed to see and hear to quiet his doubts. He brought his doubts to Jesus, and Jesus brought faith. This exchange is not exclusive to Thomas; it is available to us as well. Shame will tell you to bury your doubts and continue marching. Fear will ask you to act on your doubts and abandon your faith. Knowledge will tell you that you can find all the answers elsewhere. Jesus requests that you give your doubts to him. They do not scare or frighten him. He confidently knows how to answer and lovingly guide you through anything you can throw at him.

What is your tendency with your doubts? Is it shame and fear, or knowledge and communion with Jesus?

Dependable

You can't trust a gossiper with a secret;
they'll just go blab it all.
Put your confidence instead in a trusted friend,
for he will be faithful to keep it in confidence.
PROVERBS 11:13 TPT

God created us to be in relationship with him and with each other. Women tend to be especially relational, both to our advantage and to our harm. Some of the deepest wounds can come from other women, especially sharp, arrow-like words that strike deep. Children merely need a good game of tag and quick question to form friendships; it feels a lot harder to make new friends as we grow. That's why a good friend is such a treasure.

One trait of good friends is their dependability. Can those around you rely on you? Are you trustworthy? The Bible talks a lot about our words and their power. A woman of God will value the dependable trait and will strive for it in her relationships. God has proven to be dependable toward us, and we should mirror this in our relationships with other people. When trust is built, a wonderful friendship can flourish. Perhaps there are situations where we need to confess something to restore a relationship, or forgive someone who hurt us. We need to be dependable friends.

How can you turn away from gossip and turn toward being a dependable friend today?

Content

I know what it is to be in need, and I know what it is to have plenty. I have learned the secret of being content in any and every situation, whether well fed or hungry, whether living in plenty or in want.

PHILIPPIANS 4:12 NIV

We often attribute contentment with squashing the desire to have more. It is easily linked with being thankful, a good quality to possess as a believer. But what if we took contentment one step further? What if we exalted our lack, because in that lack we had confidence that we would see more of Christ? Paul doesn't list situations like having a smaller TV or making fewer shopping trips as the situations in which he has learned contentment. He lists real, stomach-gnawing hunger.

Elsewhere in Scripture, he talks about being beaten to near death, being shipwrecked, being abandoned by friends. Still, he found contentment in those situations because Christ was sufficient to cover any deficit. His joy did not swell on the unreliable waves of his circumstances or possessions; his deepest joy was Christ. The contentment message of being happy with what you have is good, but it's not enough. With contentment, we must learn to be at peace with what we do not have, knowing that in all those areas, Christ is enough.

What does being content mean to you?

Generous

Give freely and become more wealthy;
be stingy and lose everything.
The generous will prosper;
those who refresh others
will themselves be refreshed.
PROVERBS 11:24-25 NLT

Get-rich-quick systems and businesses who promise to change your life with wealth abound in our world. Here in Proverbs, the author is not presenting another pyramid scheme. He is pointing out that to be a Christian means to be generous. It should be a defining quality.

Have you ever met a family that has a physical feature that defines them? For instance, you see that fiery red hair, and you can say, "Oh, that's Jim's kid." As God's kids, we should mark our lives with generosity. This is not limited to money. It should penetrate all areas of our lives: our time, our money, our resources. The gospel's change in our lives takes us from living with a tight fist to an open hand. It enables us to release the grasp we have on all our assets and act in the same manner of our Savior, generously giving all.

Is generosity a marker in your life for others? Or do you hold a tight grasp on what you have?

Grace

> *By grace you have been saved through faith.*
> *And this is not your own doing; it is the gift of God.*
>
> EPHESIANS 2:8 ESV

This word *grace* gets thrown around in Christian culture more often than a baseball in an extra-inning game. With all that traction, it can easily lose its power, becoming commonplace to us. Far from common, grace is the factor of our religion that sets us apart from all others. In man's great pursuit (and rejection) of God, many avenues and religions have formed. Islam, Jehovah's Witness, Latter-day Saints, Buddhism, and on and on the list goes. What sets Christianity apart?

The key is grace. Grace is not us working our way to God. Grace is not God measuring us to see if we meet the standard of holiness. Grace is a gift that we don't deserve, given to us by God. Christianity is the only religion that makes it not about what we do and all about what God does. What he does for us is summed up in this precious word—grace. Let its power transform you today as you dwell on this word.

Has the word grace *become commonplace to you?*

Informed

> "Well did Isaiah prophesy of you hypocrites, as it is
> written, 'This people honors me with their lips, but their
> heart is far from me; in vain do they worship me, teaching
> as doctrines the commandments of men.' You leave the
> commandment of God and hold to the tradition of men."
>
> MARK 7:6-8 ESV

In this passage, Jesus is calling out the hypocrisy of the well-learned Pharisees. When we become believers, we get to know God better through study of his Word and prayer. This leads some to pursue higher education in the Bible, known as the study of theology. For those of us that don't go that route, there is still an abundance of books by Christian authors, pastors, and teachers on all areas of knowledge about God.

These resources in and of themselves are not bad, and many can be helpful to our growth. However, in our quest to gain knowledge of God, let us not lose the intimacy of a relationship with God. Striving to be informed is not a bad pursuit, but like many pursuits, it can become an idol. In a marriage, if you only focus on facts about a person, you are more of a biographer and less of a lover. To have intimacy, one must pursue experience, give time, and express vulnerability. Let us not forget that we are not just participating in a religion of research. We are pursuing a relationship with the God of creation.

In the pursuit of knowledge, have you made Jesus more of a professor than a friend?

Legacy

We will not hide these truths from our children;
we will tell the next generation
about the glorious deeds of the LORD,
about his power and his mighty wonders.

PSALM 78:4 NLT

There is a song by a popular Christian artist that talks about legacy. She sings poetically about how when she is old, she hopes that the one thing that her children and those around her remember is that she treasured Jesus above all else. When considering legacy, many people focus on material possessions or their life's work. As Christians, the legacy we should seek is just what the singer describes. May those who meet us say that we treasured Jesus more than anything else.

We have an enemy, Satan, whose purpose is to steal, kill, and destroy. He wants nothing more than to steal this legacy from you and destroy any testimony you may have. We must be careful keepers of our legacy. It is helpful to step back and to look at our lives. What would your kids, friends, or family say you treasure most? Your phone? Your career? Your pets or home decor? How are you using your assets and time? What occupies your thought life the most? These self-evaluating questions can help us to see if Jesus is our legacy, or if we've been deceived.

Prayerfully consider the questions listed above.

Leader

He shepherded them according
to the integrity of his heart,
And guided them with his skillful hands.

PSALM 78:72 NASB

You might not view yourself as one, but most of us are leaders. If you are a mom, you are leading your kids. You might not hold a title at work, but others still see your example. At church, you are a woman of God, and that is known and observed by all around you. There are so many layers to your relationships, and you are called to be a leader in at least one.

In Psalms, we are told that leadership starts on the inside. You cannot lead others if you are not tending to your own soul. What you do in unseen moments ripples out to all the seen moments of influence, whether you are influencing one or thousands. We must be women who cultivate a deeper life of prayer, worship, and time in the Word. Through these and other spiritual disciplines, our inner life will flourish with wisdom. From this flourishing, we can properly lead those around us. Remember, you cannot pour from an empty cup. Let Christ fill you if you desire to pour into the lives of those around you today.

Do you tend to your inner life, or do you ignore spiritual disciplines while leading from an empty cup?

Innocent

Your obedience is known to all, so that I rejoice over you,
but I want you to be wise as to what is good and innocent
as to what is evil.

ROMANS 16:19 ESV

There are people specifically trained to identify counterfeit money. They teach that the best way to identify a counterfeit is not to study all the various counterfeit bills or methods, but to study and know the actual one inside and out. Learn its textures, images, and what specific markers it has. Then, you will have a better chance of catching a fake later.

In today's verse, Paul gave some of his final words from prison to the church in Rome. In the previous two verses, he spoke of false teachers attempting to deceive the church. Paul's exhortation is to not concentrate heavily on the false teaching. Instead, he encourages believers to do the same as those who identify counterfeit bills. To be innocent to the false teachings that are coming, we do not spend our time diving deeply into them. We need to instead drink deeply of the living water, the Word of God. We need to know the truth: how it feels, how it looks, how it applies. Don't worry about deception; make yourself wise in the knowledge of the Lord.

Do you worry about getting caught up in false teaching?
How can you focus on truth more than false teaching this week?

Healthy

"I will restore you to health and heal your wounds,"
declares the Lord.

JEREMIAH 30:17 NIV

The Hebrew word *shalom* is more than a greeting. It means wholeness, completeness. Shalom is the perfect word to express the desire of the Father's heart for your life. We are not made to live fragmented lives, with our spirituality neatly tied up in our Sunday morning box, our families in another box, our sex lives in another box, our physical health in another, and so on.

God created us for wholeness. When he says he desires healing and health for you, it's more than just a physical thing. Emotional, spiritual, physical—God can restore it all. He wants us to be whole, integrated people who worship and bring glory to him with our whole lives, not fragments. The power of the Holy Spirit will bring down the walls you have between the sections of your life and enable you to live a healthy, vibrant life that flows naturally from your spirit.

What areas of your life are you boxing off from Jesus? Ask Jesus to show you how to pursue holistic, healthy spirituality today.

Pleasant

The LORD is all I need, he takes care of me.
My share in life has been pleasant;
my part has been beautiful.

PSALM 16:5-6 NCV

If you've read Scripture's accounts of David's life, you might scratch your head a bit at this phrase he writes in Psalm 16. Sure, he is considered one of the great kings of Israel and called "a man after God's own heart." However, there are accounts of him being on the run and hunted for years, multiple attempts on his life, the loss of his first-born child, adultery, murder, and a mess of a family life with his grown kids. How could his share have been pleasant amidst all that pain?

The answer is that David considered his inheritance, his lot in life, to be God himself. He is writing here that his focus is not on the circumstances, but on the Lord. The presence of God in his life is what made his life a pleasant life. Can you say the same about your life? When you look back through the hard times and the good times, do you see the presence of God as being evident and good in your life? Jesus is our inheritance, the greatest treasure, and the source of having a pleasant life.

Do you consider the presence of God as pleasant in your life?

Motivated

God demonstrates his own love for us in this:
While we were still sinners, Christ died for us.
ROMANS 5:8 NIV

Our motivations are the inner reasons behind the things we do. Beneath every one of your actions, there is a motive, whether good or bad. God's actions have motives, too, and one of them is you. Brimming with love and compassion for you, Jesus walked the road to the cross. It was love that motivated him to let the Romans nail his hands and feet down. It was his perfect passion for you that sent him through the hours of pain and separation from the Father. It was his desire to see you restored to peace with himself and the Father, and he kept wanting it until his last breath.

This was the motivation—you. No length was too far for the Father to go to restore you to himself. And while the Father was overflowing with the motivation of love, you were exiled from him, lost in your sin, and in rebellion of the very love that wanted to save you. This is the greatest love story ever told, this motivation of a father who stopped at nothing to bring his children home.

In your relationship with God, do you see the overflowing love he has demonstrated toward you?

Mindful

I will remember the deeds of the Lord;
yes, I will remember your miracles of long ago.
I will consider all your works and meditate
on all your mighty deeds.

PSALM 77:11-12 NIV

In an understandable pushback against modern spirituality, some Christians have abandoned the spiritual discipline of meditation and mindfulness. Scripture, however, mentions meditation over sixty times. It is a worthwhile discipline to meditate on Scripture and to focus our minds on the things of Christ. For a Christian, meditation is remembrance. When we slow down, command our souls to focus on Christ, and remember the goodness of his mighty deeds, our lives are changed.

Studies show that anxiety and stress are lessened by meditation. Imagine that discipline coupled with the power of God's beautiful Word and a focus on his presence! When we meditate, we acknowledge that God's presence is a current reality. We align our souls with the truth of Scripture, bringing ourselves joy and peace. Take today's Scripture and meditate on it. Break it down; what deeds of the Lord can you remember in your life? What miracles have you experienced? How has God worked in your life? What are his mighty deeds? How might this knowledge change your current mental state? Find peace in the presence of God.

How can you acknowledge that the presence of God is near?

Principled

*Since the creation of the world God's invisible qualities—
his eternal power and divine nature—have been clearly
seen, being understood from what has been made,
so that people are without excuse.*

ROMANS 1:20 NIV

Take some time today to read the entire chapter of Romans 1. Paul is setting up a long letter explaining that the gospel is for both Jews and Gentiles. In the first chapter, he expounds upon the state of humanity. He talks about how men denied God, even though, as today's verse says, his presence and power have always been visible.

Without a spine, the body crumbles. Without a worldview, a person is drawn into all sorts of sin. Tossed like the wind, there is no telling what direction you will head if you do not have a biblical worldview. This means that what God says needs to be the spinal cord, the guiding direction for your life. This makes you a person who is not led astray by what others say or even by the own sinful desires of her own heart, but rather a principled woman who stands firm on truth. The strength of God is available to you if you choose to align your life with God's way and his Word. Feeling weak in some areas? Ask God for an adjustment this morning.

Do you base your principles and decisions on the Word of God or your own heart?

Positive

*Whatever is true, whatever is honorable, whatever is
just, whatever is pure, whatever is pleasing, whatever is
commendable, if there is any excellence and if there is
anything worthy of praise, think about these things.*

PHILIPPIANS 4:8 ESV

What is the opposite of positive? Negative. And in what area
of our lives does negativity tend to run wild? Our thought life.
As women, we can struggle with a wide variety of negative
thoughts. Relationships, body image, self-esteem, our abilities—
it seems the enemy wants us to run a never-ending treadmill of
doubt and envy.

It's time to step off the machine. In Romans, the Bible speaks
of renewing our minds to be like Christ's. Here in Philippians,
Paul also gives us some ammunition to fight with when these
thoughts come. You can work through this Scripture as step-
by-step instructions. First, identify your negative thought. Then
ask, is it true? What does the Bible say about the matter? Is it
honoring of yourself, of God, or of others? Does it promote a
fair assessment? Is it from the Spirit, and is it holy? Continue
through the verse. Use Scripture to find positivity. This practice,
and the Holy Spirit's guidance, help us step off the treadmill of
negative thoughts and walk in pace with him.

What negative thoughts repeat themselves in your mind?

Maturity

Solid food is for the mature, who by constant use have trained themselves to distinguish good from evil.

HEBREWS 5:14 NIV

From sports to the arts to career progression, when someone wants to get better at their craft, they practice. They train. They put in the work, and this enables them to grow, learn, and become better at whatever they are working on.

The same is true of our Christian walk. In today's Scripture, solid food and milk represent spiritual food. Just as a child begins on milk and progresses to steaks and vegetables as they mature, Christians are to progress. Protection from false teaching comes through growing in knowledge of the Word of God. It comes through being in his presence in the good times so that you know what his voice sounds like in the hard times. The only way to discern between good and evil is by the power of the Holy Spirit and the wielding of his Word. Start training yourself for maturity in Christ. One way to train is to memorize Scripture. This embeds God's Word in your soul for times when you need it the most.

What are some other ways to train for maturity?

Patient

I waited patiently for the LORD;
and He inclined to me, and heard my cry.

PSALM 40:1 NKJV

We live in a fast-food culture. We are growing more and more accustomed to having our wants and needs met as instantaneously as possible. Couple that with the fact that we are also living in a culture that despises suffering, and you have a recipe for impatience. Our desire for comfort insists that we not sit in the discomfort of a God who doesn't answer the way we want or as quickly as we want. This makes us push back against a God who convicts when we want validation. In many ways, our culture trains us against godliness instead of for it.

We are to be women who wait patiently on God. We do this because we trust in him and his timing and will obey him over our human desires. God is near. God is listening. Keep your heart in the posture of openness toward him and ask for extra patience if you are waiting on him today. Waiting is not a passive game; it is an active action that is focused completely on the Lord.

What are you patiently waiting for today?

Meaningful

*Whether you eat or drink, or whatever you do,
do everything for the glory of God.*

1 CORINTHIANS 10:31 NRSV

A woman once said that when it comes to home decor, she only fills her house with meaningful items. The temptation is ever-present to grab the latest trendy thing off the shelves at the local department store. Instead, she tries to be intentional about what she puts in her home, from the art on the walls to the vase on a shelf. She asks herself if the items bring her joy. If they are meaningful to her in some way, then the items get to stay.

This selection is the key to living a purposeful life. There is not room for everything; too many things create clutter and chaos. A life of purpose is a life that has picked out the meaningful things that give God the glory to prioritize. This doesn't necessarily mean flashy or big things, as even ordinary events can honor God. This means analyzing our schedules, our money, our goals, and our hobbies to see what brings meaning to us and glory to God, and what we should probably kick to the curb.

How can you create a life of purpose by analyzing your habits?

Mentor

*Show yourself in all respects to be a model of good works,
and in your teaching show integrity, dignity, and sound
speech that cannot be condemned, so that an opponent
may be put to shame, having nothing evil to say about us.*

TITUS 2:7-8 ESV

In this chapter, several people are instructed in who to teach
and how to teach them. In Titus's case, he is instructed to
set up mentorship-type systems amongst the believers. This
is important today, too. It is vital for believers to be a part of
a local, Bible-believing church. It is equally as important for
believers to go deeper into that body, mentoring and being
mentored by fellow believers.

A mentorship does not have to be complicated. A woman who is
a few steps ahead of you in her walk and life can be an excellent
mentor to pray with you and share life's cares with. Likewise,
a woman who is a few steps behind you could be looking for
support that you can give. God has placed each of us, and
people we are around, for a reason. Be poured into and pour
out as well.

*Prayerfully think about who you could mentor, or be mentored
by, and pursue that relationship. If you already have this set up,
thank God for those people and pray for them today.*

February

"Don't be dejected and sad,
for the joy of the LORD is your strength!"

NEHEMIAH 8:10 NLT

Honest

> *There is a time to cry and a time to laugh.*
> *There is a time to be sad and a time to dance.*
>
> ECCLESIASTES 3:4 NCV

When a new year comes, we are supposed to feel energized for a new beginning. Valentine's Day tells us we are supposed to feel loved. Christmas begs us to be full of joy and happiness. Holidays are markers of time that are attached to certain assumed feelings, and when we don't feel that particular way, we feel wrong.

Christianity can be the same way. If you are saved, shouldn't you feel a certain way all the time? That's not what God says. God understands the complexity of your emotions; he's the one who made you to feel them. He created us to have times of mourning, times of joy, and time for everything in between. It's beneficial for us and our walk with Christ to stop forcing ourselves to feel a certain way or to hide our emotions. Instead, we can be honest about them before the Lord. God welcomes you to bring every emotion you may have to him; he wants you to. He didn't create us to be robots, but to be humans in communion with him. God invites all your being to be with him today, no matter how you are feeling. Won't you come?

Do you try to hide your emotions from God?

Incredible

The heavens tell of the glory of God;
And their expanse declares the work of His hands.
Day to day pours forth speech,
And night to night reveals knowledge.

PSALM 19:1-2 NASB

If you desire a transformed life, learn to be a woman who lives in awe of God. Awe and wonder are qualities often missing from our modern lives. Search engines, just a tap away, provide all the answers we need. Social media and TV pour the headlines into us day and night, and even GPS systems leave no room for wandering.

We listen intently to all these sources, but when was the last time you took a moment to listen to what is being said in nature? Psalms tells that, day and night, things are being revealed about God through the heavens and the works of his hands. Perhaps we have become so accustomed to receiving our knowledge elsewhere that we don't even hear it. How amazing that there are constantly things being said about God! It never gets old or runs out. He is endless and wonderful, and our lives are transformed when we stop to listen to the praise of his glory.

How can you listen today to what is being said about our
incredible God?

Jubilant

May the righteous be glad and rejoice before God;
may they be happy and joyful.

PSALM 68:3 NIV

Who is looking for a reason to celebrate? If you love a good party, here is the perfect reason to rejoice. The Christian life should be one marked by celebration and joy. Our God is an awesome God who has done great things for us! When you remember the ways the Lord has worked in your life, it's not always appropriate to keep them to yourself. God's movement in your life and in the world around you is joyful to you, and it can be great encouragement for others.

The stories we live through are not meant just for our ears. They should be shouted and often retold, revealing the great things God has done. Joy is contagious. When you are full of the joy of the Lord, others will catch on as well. You never know who needs to hear of his powerful working. They may be desperate for God to move in the same way, or maybe they need to hear that they are not alone. Rejoice, declare, and exclaim the works of the Lord!

Who can you encourage with contagious joy?

Known

He knows our frame;
He remembers that we are dust.
PSALM 103:14 NKJV

Much of human behavior can be linked to the deep desire within all of us to be known. The relationships we treasure are the ones that offer the intimacy of being known. Even the closest human relationships will fall short, but with Christ, we can be fully known. To some, that might be terrifying. For a believer, it can be comforting.

Christ came to earth and became God made human—really, fully human. He has been tempted in all the ways we have been tempted. He has been hurt, hungry, and thirsty. He has felt pain, loneliness, and joy. There is no aspect of the human experience that Jesus protected himself from. Though he did not sin, he still knows everything about being human. This knowledge encourages us because we know are never alone in our experience. Jesus can relate. No matter your experience, he sympathizes with you and wants to know you completely. There is no need to hold back or be ashamed. Let yourself be known by the one who knows.

Do you try to hold back aspects of yourself from Christ, or do you allow yourself the joy and intimacy of being fully known?

Forthright

I delivered to you as of first importance what I also received: that Christ died for our sins in accordance with the Scriptures, that he was buried, that he was raised on the third day in accordance with the Scriptures.

1 CORINTHIANS 15:3-4 ESV

Being forthright means being upfront and clear. If you've been a Christian for any amount of time, you've probably heard the word *doctrine*. Doctrine refers to the interpretation and teachings of Scripture. Different believers have different views on certain aspects of Scripture and how it is to be interpreted.

Though discussions about doctrine are not bad, we should not let them be distracting or divisive. Scripture is clear on many things, the most important being the gospel. Since Scripture is clear on it, we should be, too. Because of the fall of man, all of us sin. There is no way we can work our way back to a right relationship with God. Jesus came to dwell among us, fully man and fully God. He lived a sinless life and was crucified to atone for our sins. Because of his death and his resurrection, every human can now be in right standing before God through belief in Jesus. We have access to peace with God through Christ. That is the good news, the gospel! The love of God and his desire for peace with us is one thing we can all be forthright about.

Do you feel like the gospel is clear or muddy to you?

Exciting

*Since the world began,
no ear has heard and no eye has seen a God like you,
who works for those who wait for him!*

ISAIAH 64:4 NLT

Being a believer is not just another title to throw on the list of roles you hold. It should be a completely life-changing experience, affecting all areas of your reality. The Christian life is quite the adventure for the woman who submits herself to God's will. God gives each of us specific spiritual gifts; have you discovered yours? Looking into this can bring clarity and vitality to your life. Next, take God at his word. There are so many areas where we are asked to have big faith. If you want to see God move mountains, you must have faith.

Lastly, pray specifically, and keep track. When you write down your prayers and go back to look at them, you will find a pathway through all the ways God showed up in your life. It's thrilling to see God moving and answering our prayers. If you feel like your walk with Christ is just another title, maybe it's time to do some self-examination.

What steps of faith do you think Jesus is asking you to take?

Enduring

Love bears all things, believes all things,
hopes all things, endures all things.

1 Corinthians 13:7 esv

How is bearing all things different from believing all things? The words used for the term *bearing* seem to imply more of a temporary situation. Think of it like patience in the moment of trial. Enduring all things is a long-term situation. It's not jumping ship on the relationship when things get difficult.

Now, it must be said that in cases of verbal, sexual, or physical abuse, you are not being asked to endure. But in the case of difficult relationships, we are asked to endure in love with our brothers and sisters in Christ. When they struggle with sin, when they get physically ill, when they hit hard times, the Bible asks us to endure. We display the love of Christ by the way we stick around when the going gets tough. We put other people first, serving them as Christ would, when we endure some painful situations to see them through. This is the love that Christ displays toward us. True love will not look like fairy tales we have read or movies we have watched. Biblical love is far more weathered, and far more beautiful.

Who are you enduring in love with?

Deliberate

Commit to the LORD whatever you do,
and he will establish your plans.

PROVERBS 16:3 NIV

You've heard it lamented before. "Time flies!" "Where did the time go?" "Time just got away from me." Phrases like these have probably fallen from your own lips. The older we get, the more we realize how fleeting our time on this earth is. For some, that idea can be paralyzing. For Christians, let us take it as a reminder to live each day for Christ. Our time on earth is short, and we can make each moment count by being intentional about how we use our time.

Each new day is a gift from God, a blank slate to be used, not just to hurry around getting things done, but to look up from our rush and see the opportunities to bring God glory in our everyday life. It takes a shift in mindset, a release, to say, "God, not my will, but yours." He has plans for your day. Have you asked him what they might be? Let us be intentional, deliberate women who submit their days to God, looking for opportunities to know him and make him known in each ordinary instance.

Do you have room in your schedule for God's plans?

Edifying

Each of us should please our neighbors for their good,
to build them up.

ROMANS 15:2 NIV

Have you ever been through the process of building a house?
The building of a home is never a quick thing. There are many
workers and many layers, and it takes time to build a house that
is going to last. In the New Testament, the word for edification
literally means "the building of a house."

Many times in Scripture, we are referred to as a temple of God.
All believers together form this temple. We are given spiritual
gifts so that we can edify, or build up, the temple. Edification is
far more than just a nice word. The gifts that the body has been
given range widely, and the disciplines we can engage in vary. All
can build up those in our community. This helps other believers
progress spiritually. It can be a slow and laborious process,
much like building a real house. In the end however, the work is
always worth it, and you have something that will last.

What gifts have you been given to edify the body of Christ? Do you
see your gifts as beneficial for others, or do you only use them for
yourself?

Focused

He said, "Come." So Peter got out of the boat,
started walking on the water, and came toward Jesus.

MATTHEW 14:29 NRSV

The miracle of Peter walking on the water never gets old. Today, let's zoom in on the aspect of the story found in Matthew 14:29-30. Jesus affirms Peter's desire to get out of the boat and walk toward him. Peter was one of the closest people to Jesus; he had left everything to follow Jesus and become one of the twelve. On top of that, Peter was also a part of the inner circle of three disciples that knew Jesus best.

Here, Peter asked for more. He asked for a deeper experience with Jesus. He asked for the faith to step into a crazy storm toward his Savior, and Jesus told him to come. As Peter steps out onto the waves, his eyes are locked on Jesus. However, in the following verse, Peter shifts his focus to the waves towering above him, and that's when he begins to sink. Perhaps you have heard the hymn "Turn Your Eyes Upon Jesus." Whatever miracle you are walking toward, whatever step of faith you need to take, focus on Christ alone today.

What are your eyes focused on?

Reward

This light momentary affliction is preparing for us an
eternal weight of glory beyond all comparison, as we
look not to the things that are seen but to the things that
are unseen. For the things that are seen are transient, but
the things that are unseen are eternal.

2 CORINTHIANS 4:17-18 ESV

Perhaps your instinct is to scoff when you read the first line of this passage. *Light and momentary?* you may think. How can he possibly know how heavy and ongoing your hardships are? Suffering can leave us weary, and no one is immune to it. But Paul knows what it means to suffer. In the New Testament, he gives quite the resume regarding the topic. You can check out that resume by reading chapter 11 in 2 Corinthians.

If you think that Paul is underestimating your affliction, then you can guarantee that he is underestimating the goodness of the reward to come as well. If these trials light trials prepare us for eternal glory beyond what we can imagine, the heavy trials, the longsuffering hurts, imagine what they are doing! Although our time on this earth is not all hard things, the divine rewards that we are promised lie in the age to come. It is important to remember this as we navigate hardships: light or heavy, short or long.

Is your focus more on here and now, or are you living for the age
to come?

Respite

Perfect, absolute peace surrounds those
whose imaginations are consumed with you;
they confidently trust in you.

ISAIAH 26:3 TPT

There is a place you can go when you are weary in your soul. Perhaps the storms have beaten too hard, and the wounds have cut too deep. When you can't lift what is in front of you, when one more step feels impossible, lift your head and look. Turn to Jesus. Long and elaborate prayers not required, and no prerequisites are needed. Just say his name—Jesus. That sweet, powerful name. He is near. His presence surrounds you, bringing comfort and strength. Most of all, you are safe.

Lay down your armor; let down your walls. You are safe in his presence. You can be your true self, for he formed your truest self. He will never turn you away, never reject you. Where else can you find this kind of promise? Who else can offer us peace? He himself is peace. Your soul will not be at rest until you find rest in Christ. He offers it freely. There is rest for the weariest of people. Just say his name.

Are you finding rest in Jesus, or are you searching for it elsewhere?

Significance

We are his workmanship,
created in Christ Jesus for good works,
which God prepared beforehand,
that we should walk in them.

EPHESIANS 2:10 ESV

The search for significance is embedded into the soul of every human. At some point or another, soul-searching questions arise. "Who am I, and why am I here?" Many people spend their lives searching for the answer, looking in all the wrong places. What makes our lives significant?

We have been created by a loving God and placed into this specific point in history. But we are not the hero of this story. God created us in his image. He created us to bring him glory. He placed us in our families, in this year, in this moment, for his glory. God is central to the story. Our lives have significance when we use them for God's glory. We are most fulfilled, most satisfied, and most happy when Jesus is on the throne in our lives instead of us. It seems counter to every self-help book on significance. It is God who works all things together in the end, and if we don't join him in that purpose, it is only then that our lives are meaningless.

Ask God how you can partner with him today.

Love

This is how God showed his love to us:
He sent his one and only Son into the world
so that we could have life through him.

1 JOHN 4:9 NCV

Christmas barely has one foot out the door when retail stores start filling their shelves with another red theme. The scarlet and green of Christmas shift into the red and pink of Valentine's Day, hearts abounding where trees once stood. Valentine's Day can evoke a lot of emotions other than love in people's hearts, and perhaps in yours. For some, it's a reminder of their loneliness: of pain, heartache, or abandonment. We are made for relationships, and when those relationships break, the wounds are deep.

If we remember Saint Valentine, for whom the holiday is named, his life can point us to the true meaning of love. Saint Valentine was an early Christian martyr. He gave his life for beliefs in Christ. Though the exact details of his service to the early church are debated, it is clear that he was martyred. Saint Valentine and Jesus both displayed love for us, not by handing us flowers or chocolates, but by laying down their lives in love. 1 John has a lot to say about love, and it's clear that true love lays down its life. God, who is love, has laid down his life for you. That's the most beautiful, love-filled message you could receive today.

How has God demonstrated his love toward you?

Reliable

The Lord is faithful;
he will strengthen you
and guard you from the evil one.

2 THESSALONIANS 3.3 NLT

The entire Bible speaks to this theme: God is faithful. It's hard to count the exact number of verses that proclaim this. While we do have blatant verses, like our verse from 2 Thessalonians today, the bulk of Scripture communicates through narrative. In those narratives, from Eve to the early church, God is faithful to his people. God never goes back on his word, and he always keeps his promises.

In Genesis, you can see that he was faithful to Eve in his promise about her descendent crushing the serpent's head. He was faithful to Sarah when he told her she would have a son. He is faithful to mankind in that he has never flooded the earth in its entirety again. The list goes on and on. The hero in every one of those stories is God, and he is reliable to every person. How has God been reliable to you? He promises us that if we call on him and believe, he will save us from our sins. He promises us that there is nothing that can separate us from his love. Which promise do you need to hear today?

How can you see God being reliable in his promise?

Sober

The end of all things is at hand;
therefore, be self-controlled and sober-minded
for the sake of your prayers.

1 PETER 4:7 ESV

With this verse being written so many years ago, you might think Peter got it wrong. The end of all things has not come yet, two thousand years later! However, he isn't suggesting that he knew when the end would come. The point he is trying to make is that we now live in the church age, the last phase in the plan of redemption. The only thing that is next is Jesus' return!

With this information in mind, prayer is of the essence. Prayer is the secret weapon of the believer, an often ignored one. Our lack of understanding about prayer or inability to see the importance of it hinders us. Prayer is our privilege, and we are not to take it lightly. We believers living in this church age have the distinct privilege of the Holy Spirit living inside of us, a constant connection to God. Jesus made a way for us to have this privilege. With that in mind, let us treat it like the honor that it is. We can do this by prioritizing prayer in our lives, by taking God at his word, and by looking for him to move through our prayers.

What role does prayer play in your life?

Tactful

*Speaking the truth in love, we are to grow up in every
way into him who is the head, into Christ, from whom the
whole body, joined and held together by every joint with
which it is equipped, when each part is working properly,
makes the body grow so that it builds itself up in love.*

EPHESIANS 4:15-16 ESV

It is clear in Scripture that sin and God do not coexist. God is
holy, and in him is no sin at all. As believers, we are called to
be holy as God is holy. Armed with this knowledge, we often
set out with good intentions but end up sinning against our
sisters and brothers when we try to confront or point out sin
in the lives of others. As Ephesians states, we are a body that is
to grow and be built up together. We need each other, and we
need to be able to call out sin in one another's lives.

However, in our quest for holiness, we often leave out the "in
love" part. We have a passion to speak truth, but if it is not
done in love, we are just a clanging noise that hurts others' ears.
We do more harm than good to the body of Christ if we slice
and dice with our words, tearing down our fellow believers.
Dear sister, let us make sure that if we feel the nudge to speak
into another life, especially regarding sin, that we do so with
the love of Holy Spirit completely blanketing our words.

Do you struggle with speaking truth in love?

Splendid

On the glorious splendor of your majesty,
and on your wondrous works, I will meditate.
PSALM 145:5 NLT

At the beginning of a relationship, the two involved are so enamored with each other they gush with praise. Sometimes, it gets old being around them because it seems like their new partner can do no wrong. As flawed humans, this honeymoon phase wears off, and hopefully a healthy balance is found.

However, there is no end to the good things we could say about God. The honeymoon phase should never wear off, because we will never be able to express all the good things he has done. He is a magnificent God. There are angels in heaven whose one job and purpose is to declare these things for eternity! We serve an awesome God. With that in mind, when was the last time you dwelt on how splendid God was? When did you last share his greatness with someone else? Don't let the newness of your faith wear off. God is still moving, still great, and there are still many things to be declared about him.

What can you share about the splendor of God today?

Trustworthy

Those who know your name trust in you,
for you, LORD, have never forsaken those who seek you.
PSALM 9:10 NIV

Trust is something that is built. It can be given freely at first, but it continues by being earned. Trusting in God requires us to know God. We build that trust through relationship with him. As we walk with the Lord, he proves himself faithful and trustworthy time and time again. We can start with the basic knowledge, as spoken of in the Scriptures, that he is trustworthy, but it is through experience with God that this knowledge makes it way to the depths of our heart.

If we trust him in the small, daily matters, we will build a foundation that will keep us steady when the bigger trials come. We can build this by examining where we have a hard time giving up control. Do you struggle with giving because finances always feel too tight? Do you have a tight grip on your appearance, afraid to let anyone see you without makeup or hair done? Does your house have to be just so to invite others in, which might hinder fostering deep relationships? Control looks different for all of us.

What do you need to release control of and develop trust in today?

Unafraid

When I saw him, I fell at his feet as though dead.
But he laid his right hand on me, saying,
"Fear not, I am the first and the last, and the living one.
I died, and behold I am alive forevermore,
and I have the keys of Death and Hades."

REVELATION 1:17-18 ESV

How often are the two words *fear not* spoken in the Bible?
Around 365 times! The message is clear. As believers, we are
called to live our lives unafraid. In today's passage from the
book of Revelation, it is Jesus who says, "Fear not." Following
that, he gives us three points on why we can live unafraid.

First, he is the first and the last. This title means that he exists,
that he always has and always will. He is gloriously eternal.
Second, he is the living one that died and is now alive. This
the hope of the resurrection. And lastly, he's got the keys! The
person who has the keys to the car has the power to start the
car. Likewise, Jesus has the keys over sin and death; he's in
control. This is the mighty God we serve: the one who has
conquered death, is in control, is outside of time, and will reign
forever more. These are all reasons we do not have to fear.

How does Christ having the keys give you confidence?

Steadfast

The steadfast love of the LORD never ceases;
his mercies never come to an end;
they are new every morning;
great is your faithfulness.

LAMENTATIONS 3:22-23 ESV

Steadfast means to be devoted, firm and unwavering. The negative version of steadfast could be stubborn. We might relate more to being stubborn, which in our view is someone who refuses to budge from something even in the face of a good defense. So, what is God stubborn about?

God is stubborn in his love for you and his desire to have you reunited with him. In the Bible, Satan is called the accuser, and it says that he accuses us constantly, dragging up our shortfalls and our sins to both God and to ourselves. Jesus is constant as well; he is constantly praying for us and constantly reminding God of salvation through the cross. God doesn't need reminding because he is forgetful or unwilling, but Jesus is our great mediator. They made this plan together, and they rejoice together as it is fulfilled. Even though the facts of your sin might be true, the power of the cross speaks a better truth. If God is stubborn in his love for you, nothing can change that. Nothing can separate you from it. Let's rejoice in the steadfast love of the Lord!

How do you feel about God's steadfast love?

Sufficient

By a single offering he has perfected for all time those who are being sanctified.

HEBREWS 10:14 ESV

In women's ministries, you will often see the self-esteem-based message, "You are enough." While written with good intentions, this message only gives us a temporary boost to a long-term problem. If it is based on ourselves, it will fall short because we inevitably fall short. We are not perfect.

We do not have to be enough. Jesus is enough. In Christ, we are enough because he is. Jesus is sufficient in every way. He came to earth and lived a perfect life in the face of every temptation we face. He fulfilled humanity's desperate need for a deliverer and built the bridge between us and God. He restored to us peace with God, and he went further and equipped us with the Holy Spirit to live help us live fulfilled lives. If you struggle with perfectionism or finding strength within yourself, this word is for you. Stop. Because Jesus is enough, we don't have to be. Rest in the sufficiency of your Savior and friend.

How does Jesus being enough bring you rest?

Unique

Now, O Lord, you are our Father;
we are the clay, and you are our potter;
we are all the work of your hand.

Isaiah 64:8 esv

Our God is a highly creative God. All you have to do is look around at creation—the colors, the shapes, the textures—to know this. See the intricate design on the deepest sea creature, the most brilliant colors on the tiniest of bugs. God doesn't hit a creative block.

He has the same imagination in our design. He is the creative potter, molding and shaping each of our individual lives to be a masterpiece. He has to cut and take some away, sometimes remold or reform, sometimes spend long amounts of time on one area. God knows your strength and weaknesses. He knows your fears and your desires. He knows you because he formed you, and he continues to form you. We are to be women who submit to this forming, women who say, "It's your will, Lord!" and follow his lead. Then, he can use our unique gifts and makeup in the world around us. We are not just passive clay. We can be active partners with God in the shaping and formation of history itself. How exciting!

What has God called you to do?

Sustenance

*When the people of Israel saw it, they said to one another, "What is it?" They did not know what it was, and Moses said to them, "It is the bread that the L*ORD *has given you to eat."*

EXODUS 16:15 ESV

It had been a month and a half since the Israelites had left the captivity of Egypt. Though they suffered under the oppression of the pharaoh in Egypt, at this point in their freedom, many began to complain. They complained that what pharaoh gave them back in Egypt to eat was better than whatever it was they ate out in the wilderness. The next day, the Lord gave them bread that rained from heaven.

God provided for them in the wilderness, amid their complaints, in the face of bold accusations that Egypt would have been better. Every good gift we have comes from God, who has saved us from the captivity of sin and brought us into freedom. He not only provides for our physical needs, but has provided Jesus, the bread of life, to bring sustenance to our souls. We do not live in want, but in abundance.

Do you live your life longing for "Egypt," looking for your provision elsewhere?

Thoughtful

*Do not merely look out for your own personal interests,
but also for the interests of others.*

PHILIPPIANS 2:4 NASB

Being thoughtful is simple. It means thinking about what other people might be feeling or needing versus only looking out for yourself. Thoughtfulness might be simple to sum up in a sentence, but it is not simple to put into practice. We are by nature selfish people. We protect ourselves, take care of our needs, and consider our own feelings. This is not a bad thing! You are a child of God, and he wants you to be taken care of, too. Still, we must look beyond taking care of ourselves and look out for the interests of those God has placed in our circles.

Jesus set the ultimate example of this when, as described in Philippians 2, he laid down his life for us. Ask yourself, how would that make you feel? What can you do that would be encouraging to a certain person? Thoughtfulness is a form of love that seeks to uplift others and sees to their wellbeing.

God has placed the people around you for a reason. Who is he asking you to lift up today?

Studious

Keep this Book of the Law always on your lips;
meditate on it day and night, so that you may
be careful to do everything written in it.
Then you will be prosperous and successful.

JOSHUA 1:8 NIV

Does the Bible intimidate you? Be honest. It can be an intimidating book! It holds sixty-six separate books, written over thousands of years in several different literary styles. Oh, and don't forget the long genealogies, names, and places that are unfamiliar to our modern minds. Perhaps you simply don't enjoy reading or studying.

God hasn't called all of us to be career theologians, but he has asked all of us to be students of his Word. The Word of God is one of the ways God has revealed himself to mankind. It is necessary and vital to know the Word of God if you want to know God. If you feel unequipped to understand this ancient text, remember that we have the power of the Holy Spirit to reveal and discern Scripture. What a great study buddy! If Bible study intimidates you, start in a book like John. You don't have to read it; you can listen, too. The point is just to get to know the text, and through it, get to know God.

What Bible study methods do you use?

Self-Control

The grace of God has appeared that offers salvation to all people. It teaches us to say "No" to ungodliness and worldly passions, and to live self-controlled, upright and Godly lives in this present age.

TITUS 2:11-12 NIV

The classic example of self-control is the cookie in front of a kid test. You put a cookie in front of a kid. You tell them that they can have one cookie now, or if they wait till you come back, they can have five cookies. Do they have enough self-control to wait for what is to come? Of course, it depends on the kid, but what gives certain kids the will to say no to an instant cookie? It's the hope of future bounty.

For the believer, self-control is not a matter of self-empowered restraint. Self-control is powered by the grace of God. It is recognizing that God has had mercy on us, sinners though we are, and because of this grace and power, we can say no to the things that tempt us now. Because grace has bought us a future hope, we can be self-controlled women. Let us be women who recognize this truth in our lives, who know the power of grace, and rejoice at our future hope.

What does self-control look like for you?

Reflective

As in water face reflects face,
so the heart of man reflects the man.
PROVERBS 27:19 ESV

Waking up in the morning, one of the first things you may do is rub your eyes, put on your slippers, and walk down the hall to the bathroom. In the bathroom, most of us have a mirror so we can watch as we wash our faces in the morning. Before leaving the house, at work or at a restaurant, we often check our reflection in the mirror throughout the day to check our teeth or fix our hair.

In the same way you use the mirror to check your appearance, your soul's appearance is visible through the state of your heart. It's not as visible and accessible as walking past a mirror in the hallway is. God has given us the mirrors of prayer and the Bible to expose our hearts. When we slow down and spend time in his Word and in prayer, identifying the feelings and emotions we are having, we can find out the true states of ourselves. Elsewhere in Scripture, it tells us we then have a choice. We can ignore what we see and walk away, or we can respond. You might not be able to change your outward reflection, but God gives you the opportunity to change the inward one.

Have you spent time in reflection about your inner self?

March

*"Don't be afraid, for I am with you.
Don't be discouraged, for I am your God.
I will strengthen you and help you.
I will hold you up with
my victorious right hand."*

ISAIAH 41:10 NLT

Polite

Be wise in the way you act toward outsiders; make the most of every opportunity. Let your conversation be always full of grace, seasoned with salt, so that you may know how to answer everyone.

COLOSSIANS 4:5-6 NIV

Who is being referred to as outsiders in this passage? The phrase is borrowed from a Jewish phrase of the time that referred to those outside of the synagogue. In our passage, it is certainly referring to those outside of the Colossian believers. Think about your life. What "outsiders" do you interact with? For example, a wide-open field of outsiders can be the internet. What a place to try to be polite!

The exhortation for the church in Colossians is the same for believers on the internet today. You have no idea who will see the things you write and share online. Our words matter, and we should be concerned with how the things we say and the way we say them will reflect upon the gospel for others. The encouragement here is to only speak words that are full of grace. The next part of the verse talks about salt. What does salt do? It brings out the flavor of a dish. Likewise, let our conversations and speech bring out the good flavors of grace and love that the gospel so freely offers.

How can this verse help you with interactions online?

Potential

*To him who is able to do immeasurably
more than all we ask or imagine,
according to his power that is at work within us.*

EPHESIANS 3:20 NIV

Youth is for the dreamers. When we are young, many of us start out full of zeal and dreams for the future. We are told, and we believe, that we can do anything. As we grow older, disillusionment, troubles, and detours seem to abound. We often get sidetracked and settle into a different life than we anticipated. While this is not always a bad thing, with some soul-searching, some of us will find that it is bad. We have settled into comfortable lives instead of moving in the way God has asked us to do.

We got it wrong as youths. It is not us that can do anything, but God. God can do more than we can ever possibly dream up for our own lives. He wants us to partner with him in those dreams. He has the power; he has the plan. It's up to us to not cozy down into our comforts, but to be expectant and willing, asking God, "What's next?" This delights our Father's heart to hear that we want to partner with him. His potential for us is endless. Won't you join him today?

What dream has God given you?

Purity

*"Blessed are the pure in heart,
for they will see God."*

MATTHEW 5:8 NIV

What if we lived in a society that had no adultery and no murder? Would Jesus be satisfied with this? He tells us himself that the answer is no. Jesus is not content with only our outward actions being changed; he's going for our hearts. In Matthew 23. he speaks plainly to the Pharisees, chastising them for taking care of their outward appearances but ignoring their hearts. Further in Matthew 5, in Jesus' famous sermon on the mount, he addresses adultery and murder. For both, he says even lusting after a person in your heart, or being full of anger in your heart, makes you impure.

It's not enough, dear sister, to play the game of cleaning our lives. Tidy, religious lives do no good for the kingdom of God. Jesus is asking us to go deeper, to be pure in the very core of who we are. This kind of purity is only achieved by the work of the Holy Spirit in our lives.

A pure heart is one that is completely devoted to God. Are there areas of your life you are holding back?

Responsive

My heart has heard you say,
"Come and talk with me."
And my heart responds,
"Lord, I am coming."
PSALM 27:8 NLT

Have you ever wondered if God is really listening? We pray prayers or do things to get his attention. We feel discouraged when it feels like he is not close by. In today's verse, the tables feel flipped. It is God who is imploring for commune with the psalmist. The psalmist replies positively, seeking God. How did the psalmists know to respond to God? How did the psalmist respond?

In Genesis, it says that Adam walked in the garden with God in the cool of the day. Doesn't that sound delightful? An intimate stroll with your Creator, having his full ear, knowing you have all his attention. Well, dear sister, God is near. The Holy Spirit is with you, and you can walk with him anytime, anywhere. It is not God who wanders or strays; it is far too often us. But he is ever near, saying to us, "Come and talk with me." There is no game to play to get his attention; he is all ears. Won't you tell him you're coming today?

How can you draw near to God today?

Quiet

"Be still, and know that I am God.
I will be exalted among the nations,
I will be exalted in the earth!"
PSALM 46:10 ESV

Did you know that silence is a spiritual discipline? This means that silence and solitude is something we can practice regularly to help our souls be healthy. However, we live in a noisy world. It seems that as time progresses, our world only gets noisier. With more and more opportunities to be connected, we have more and more ways to drown out the voice of our Creator. If we want to live according to his will, we are in desperate need of hearing his voice.

It's surprising how loud silence can be. Many of us avoid it out of fear. Perhaps we want to avoid what will surface in us when we just stop. Perhaps it's the fear that God won't show up. Whatever is holding you back, you are commanded to practice silence. Try starting small, with just five minutes outside around the block without headphones or some quiet time in your bedroom, alone. Tell God you want to know him through silence. Jesus drew away from the crowd often to pray and be alone. Let's follow his example and get quiet before God.

What fear makes you avoid silence?

Heir

If children, then heirs, heirs of God and joint heirs with
Christ—if, in fact, we suffer with him so that we may also
be glorified with him.

ROMANS 8.17 NRSV

Today, we have a beautiful passage that speaks of the love our
Father has for us. First, there is the word *children*. We are God's
children through adoption. Though all humans are made in
God's image, those who believe in the Son are his children.
We are new creations, have had a second birth, and now are
adopted into the family of God. Being a child of God means
fellowship with God has been restored. It means that we can
access God anytime through prayer, and that bountiful mercy
is available to us. It means we can trust in our Father to give us
good gifts and to provide for our every need. Lastly, it ties into
being an heir because eternity is our inheritance.

As God's children, we have been given the right to an
inheritance with Christ. Christ's inheritance is all that is in
existence, his riches, and his glory. We are to share in that in
the age to come, but we also share in the suffering of Christ.
Though we are told the suffering is temporary, the glory is
eternal. What we endure now cannot be compared to the glory
that is to come as heirs of the Father. Praise God for this truth!

What does it mean to you to be an heir of God?

Humble

> *"Whoever exalts himself will be humbled,*
> *and whoever humbles himself will be exalted."*
> MATTHEW 23:12 ESV

Here in Matthew, Jesus presents to us another principle of the upside-down kingdom. Those who humble themselves will be exalted. Every kingdom of this world will tell you that to get ahead, you must fight your way up the ladder. These systems run on pride and self-promotion. But Jesus' way is the opposite. He asks his followers to humble themselves.

To humble yourself does not mean that you hate yourself or treat yourself poorly. Humility is thinking less of yourself. To do this, sometimes we need to be quiet. To listen, be forgiving, let go of judgment, and be gracious to others are all "easier said than done" ways of preferring others. With God, it means to confess our sins, to be quiet before him, and to pray that his will be done, not our own. Jesus, our King, was the humblest servant of all. Philippians 2 lays out for us exactly how humble he was. If our God displayed humility even to the point of losing his life, are we better than our King? No! Let us lay our lives down for others, following the humble example of Christ.

Which action listed about becoming humble stood out to you most?

Inclined

I waited patiently for the LORD;
and He inclined to me, and heard my cry.

PSALM 40:1 NKJV

There's nothing worse than getting to the end of a conversation and feeling like the other person hasn't been listening to you. It's frustrating! In Scripture, the phrase "incline your ear" is found almost eighty times. The majority of these are found in Psalms. The beauty of Psalms is that it is both the inspired Word of God and a portrayal of a vast array of emotions from man. The phrase "incline your ear" means, "Pay attention!" We often find it said from the psalmist to God, and it shows us how desperate the requests are. He is desperate for God to hear, desperate for God to respond.

Desperation, hopelessness—these are traits of a good Christian. Or are they? It is completely okay to get to the end of your rope. The question is, what are we going to do when we get there? Let us be like David and cry out to God. God's ear is inclined toward you. It's ok to ask, to wonder, to shout. The Father wants to hear from his daughter, especially in her time of need. Are you feeling desperate? Cry out to God today.

Can you relate to David's desperation?

Knowledgeable

If I speak in the tongues of men or of angels, but do not have love, I am only a resounding gong or a clanging cymbal. If I have the gift of prophecy and can fathom all mysteries and all knowledge, and if I have a faith that can move mountains, but do not have love, I am nothing.

1 CORINTHIANS 13:1-2 NIV

Some of us love a good commentary. There are those of you reading this that delight in doctrine, who get giddy at the word *theology*. If that's you, this devotion is for you. The desire to research and gain knowledge of Scripture is not a bad thing. For some of us, it is our spiritual gift. If it's your gift, that means God gave it to you and wants you to use it for his glory.

However, there is a word of caution for all of us. We can be so focused on the knowledge of God that we deny ourselves the experience of an actual relationship. Imagine you were in a relationship. You read the person's dating profile. You went back to their childhood home and looked through their scrapbooks. You read journals, traced family lineage, and talked to people they knew to find out more. Would you really know that person? The answer is no. Facts cannot replace intimacy. Intimacy means you know how that person crinkles their nose, how they take their coffee, and that their eyes get red when they cry. Intimacy requires experience. Let us not exalt knowledge and forget intimacy with God.

Are you inclined to seek knowledge of God over intimacy?

Inspiration

*All scripture is inspired by God and is useful for
teaching, for reproof, for correction, and for training in
righteousness, so that everyone who belongs to God may
be proficient, equipped for every good work.*

2 TIMOTHY 3:16-17 NRSV

While Christians may differ on some of the finer points of the
Bible, there are core beliefs that we cannot waver on. One of
those core beliefs is the inerrancy of Scripture. This means that
we believe that the Bible, all sixty-six books, is the inspired
Word of God. It was given to us by God, penned by man, for
our benefit. It is one of the ways God reveals his character to us,
so to trust it is very important.

As you can see in this verse, the Bible has many purposes. Why
does it matter that it is *inspired*? This means that the people
who wrote the Bible did not do it of their own accord, but that
the Holy Spirit, in essence, guided their pens. Though what
is written uses the vocabulary and style of the time, the Holy
Spirit is in every word. With God so intimately involved in the
Bible, we know that it is trustworthy in all that it says. When
one starts to doubt the truth of the Bible, it is a slippery slope
toward unbelief.

Have you ever considered the importance of this doctrinal truth?

Needed

Encourage each other and give each other strength,
just as you are doing now.
1 THESSALONIANS 5:11 NCV

There are days when it feels like the weight of the world falls on you. Everyone around you needs you. Children, co-workers, bosses, spouses, even the pets—everyone has a need, and that need seems to only be met by you. Those are draining days! On the flip side, sometimes the kids grow up and the nest is empty. Your spouse is away, the job is running smoothly, and it seems like no one needs what you have to offer. The first scenario can be overwhelming, the second painfully lonely.

God created us to be in relationship with one another. He created us to need each other. This will look different in different seasons for each woman, but on either side of the coin, being needed is a blessing from God. You can encourage and strengthen others and receive help as well. If you are in the overwhelmed phase, ask God to strengthen you and send you someone to encourage you as well. Maybe you need to communicate some of your own needs to another person. If you are in the lonely season, know you are not discarded or alone. God has people that he needs you to reach and encourage. Ask for his direction to them today.

Right now, which scenario do you resonate most with?

Merit

*"I am the way, the truth, and the life.
No one can come to the Father except through me."*
JOHN 14:6 NLT

Would you consider yourself a good person? In street
interviews, when people are asked about their spirituality or
eternal destination, most reply with, "Well, I'm a good person."
If we lined up all of humanity in order from most to least good,
that might be true. Most of us would assume we would be
rather high on the list. After all, compared to dictators or mass
murderers, we must be pretty good people, right?

The problem is that we are not being compared to other human
beings. The standard is the holiness of God. He is completely
perfect and without sin. When put up against that standard,
every person falls short. Fortunately, our salvation is never
based on how good we are, and we should stop acting like it
is. That is called legalism, something many of us struggle with.
Legalism is a dead-end trail of consciously or subconsciously
trying to earn favor with God based on our own merit. Jesus
said he is the way, the only way. It is on his merit alone that we
are made right with God.

Do you find yourself relying more on your merit for favor with God?

Permanent

*Our citizenship is in heaven.
And we eagerly await a Savior from there,
the Lord Jesus Christ.*

PHILIPPIANS 3:20 NIV

Many people have strong views about citizenship, aliens, and refugees. It's a heated topic in politics. Want to add a layer to the conversation? Consider this. Whatever country we live in, it is not our permanent home. In fact, the Bible refers to believers as pilgrims, or sojourners, in this present land. We aren't going to stay where we are forever. We may hold citizenship in one or more countries here on earth, but as Christians, our deepest allegiance should lie with our heavenly citizenship and to our King, Jesus.

While all this makes for good head knowledge, what does it change about our current lives on earth? How would you live differently if you acknowledged that this is not your forever home? These are important questions to consider and reflect on. As citizens of heaven, we are promised many things. For example, we are made heirs with Christ, and we will spend eternity with him.

Reflecting on your life, how does this pilgrim message change your life, your goals, and your viewpoint?

Mercy

*"Overflow with mercy and compassion for others,
just as your heavenly Father overflows
with mercy and compassion for all."*

LUKE 6:36 TPT

Who is speaking here? You may be wondering why it matters.
It is important because it affects what we believe. If you
hear a rumor about someone or read a story about them in
a newspaper, do you know them? Do you know what has
happened? No, because you are getting the information
secondhand.

We hear a lot about God. There are thousands of books written
about him as well. Though these can be helpful, what does
God say about himself? When Jesus needs to describe the
Father, how does he do it? Jesus doesn't say that God is waiting
to smite people. He doesn't describe God as being angry or
overbearing. Jesus describes the Father as "overflowing with
mercy and compassion." What a description! That is who he is,
firsthand. That is his character, straight from the source. Have
you ever felt like God was any other way? We often hold harsh
of views of God, but when Jesus speaks of his Father, he says he
is full of mercy. He is full of mercy for you. Won't you receive it?

Do you view God as being full of mercy?

Attentive

"My sheep hear my voice, and I know them, and they follow me."
JOHN 10:27 ESV

In our modern times, most of us don't have sheep. We probably don't know any shepherds. However, a lot of us have dogs. One day at the off-leash dog park, a person called out the same name as another person's dog. Apparently, there were two Sams at the park! These dogs were well-trained, because only one dog came. Both dogs knew the sound of their owner's voice, even if another voice was using the same name. They only responded to the sound of their own master. This wasn't a great achievement of the dogs; this was a result of good training on behalf of the master.

Jesus is making a similar point, only with sheep. We are the sheep, and when we hear his voice, we should follow. We need to be attentive to the voice of our master. However, it's not of our own great merit that we follow him; it's because of him. He knows us, intimately and thoroughly. Through all the noise, do you hear Jesus calling?

Do you recognize the voice of Jesus?

Beauty

*Give unto the L*ORD *the glory due to His name;*
*worship the L*ORD *in the beauty of holiness.*
PSALM 29:2 NKJV

What comes to mind when you hear the word *holiness*? Does it make you think of a strict, legalistic, religious lifestyle? This is the view that many of us have when we picture holiness. To live in holiness or worship in holiness sounds miserable, because it is so unenjoyable the way we learned it. How could David have thought that holiness was beautiful? He had a right view of it. Many of us have a backwards view, calling what is good evil and evil good; calling what is sinful beautiful and what is holy ugly.

The truth is sin is ugly. It is decaying and brings death to all it touches. The majesty and glory of God and his holiness is true beauty. We must realign our vision if we are to see this. Think of it like a blind person seeing for the first time. What a thrill and a joy to see color, mountains, birds, trees, the ocean, the face of someone they love! As believers, that is a small sampling of the joy that comes from holiness and the awe of our holy God.

What is your view on holiness?

Celebrated

This is the day that the LORD has made;
Let us rejoice and be glad in it.
PSALM 118:24 ESV

This verse is often used to encourage believers to rejoice in every day they have been given as a gift from God. Though the sentiment rings true, the greater meaning of this verse is a larger picture. The previous verses give us context to see that this verse is speaking of the day of deliverance. We know that day has come; it is when Jesus was resurrected. Interestingly, this psalm is commonly sung at Passover celebrations, which happen around the time of Easter and Lent.

At this time in March, the church is in or nearing the season of Lent, which is the period leading up to Easter. Easter usually falls between March 22nd and April 25th. As a society, we have found bountiful ways to celebrate the birth of Christ. Why do we fall short when celebrating the day we have been asked to celebrate? This year, let us find ways to overflow with abundant gladness and spread the news of this gospel day that the Lord has made for us.

How are you celebrating Easter and the good news of the resurrection? Who do you need to share the celebration with?

Coherent

Whoever looks intently into the perfect law
that gives freedom, and continues in it—
not forgetting what they have heard, but doing it—
they will be blessed in what they do.

JAMES 1:25 NIV

Let's talk about hermeneutics. Hermeneutics is the interpretation and study of biblical texts. God has given us intelligent minds to be able to know Scripture. He also has given believers the Holy Spirit to help discern the knowledge. As women of God, we are called to proper handlers of the truth. Here are a few tips on how to be a woman who studies God's Word consistently and thoroughly.

First, always start your Bible study with prayer, asking for the help of the Holy Spirit. Next, survey the book as a whole. Ask the who, what, where, when, and to whom questions. Next, observe it. Read the text in its proper context and look for words that stand out. Lastly, ask God what he wants you to do with the text. Again, pray about it!

These steps can help you tackle Scripture. Try these today with the passage in James. How did it help to enrich your study?

Changeless

*Jesus Christ is the same yesterday
and today, and forever.*

HEBREWS 13:8 NASB

Ever wondered why humans are quick to become creatures
of habit? Studies have shown that routine and habits are
comforting to our brains. With so much stimulation in the
world, it is helpful for our brains to have things that don't
change much. We are faced with countless decisions, small
and big, daily. Our brains would go into overdrive if everything
changed every night. In a sense, your brain is relying on the
habitual things in your life for comfort.

It can be like this for the believer and Christ, too. Change is
inevitable, but Jesus never changes. He is loyal to us and to
his character. This makes him a safe place for us when life is
tempestuous with change. Both good and bad change can be
draining. We can rely on Jesus to be our habitual comfort.
Sometimes, we search in other places for comfort, but they never
fulfill our needs. Lean back on Christ, who is the same since the
beginning of time, and find comfort in his presence today.

How is the unchanging nature of Christ comforting to you?

Diligent

The slacker wants it all and ends up with nothing,
but the hard worker ends up with all that he longed for.
PROVERBS 13:4 TPT

The principle of diligence versus laziness is seen throughout Proverbs. The emphasis is often on different areas of life, but the outcome is the same; the sluggard ends up with nothing while the diligent prosper. You can see this principle play out in life. Those who practice at their sport score goals. Those who work at their art create masterpieces. How can we apply it to our spiritual life?

The proverb is not calling for a striving for salvation. That is a separate matter, a gift from God that no man can achieve through diligence. However, there are many spiritual disciplines that will change our lives if we are diligent in them. Reading the Bible and prayer are the foundational two. Being accountable to other believers and plugged into a local body are others. These diligent practices, when persevered in over time, will bring good fruit. Good fruit is satisfying to us. Let us put our hands to the task that is at hand: growing in knowledge and love of the Lord, bringing his gospel to the nations.

What is God calling you to be diligent in today?

Delight

The LORD your God is in your midst,
a mighty one who will save;
he will rejoice over you with gladness;
he will quiet you by his love;
he will exult over you with loud singing.

ZEPHANIAH 3:17 ESV

What is it about a newborn baby? They haven't had enough time in the world to earn praise. They are small, helpless, and unable to control their bodily functions. But those who meet a newborn cannot help but delight in them. It is not their ability or strength that draws us to them.

In this passage, God is described as mighty. The image portrayed is that of a great warrior. He is mighty to save us. But then there is also this term delight, that he delights in us with gladness. Imagine a big, tough man cradling a newborn baby, delighting in it. That is the picture here. There is nothing about us that requires God to delight in us. But he, mighty to save, expresses love toward us in many fashions. He looks at you the way a new father looks at his newborn child—with adoration. Sometimes, we just need to lock eyes with that gaze to remember that we are loved and rejoiced over.

What comfort comes from knowing that Jesus delights in you?

Constant

Rejoice in hope,
be patient in tribulation,
be constant in prayer.
ROMANS 12:12 ESV

Verses like this can cause us to give up before we've even started. The first two commands might seem doable, but the term "constant" can be overwhelming. Constant means occurring continuously over time. Does this mean you need to quit all other endeavors, lock yourself in a prayer closet, and never come out? That is not what Paul is getting at. He is asking you to make prayer a vital, habitual part of your life.

In Scripture, we see many instances of people being constant in prayer. In Acts, when Peter is in prison, it says that the church prayed constantly for him. Prayer was vital for the early believers, and it should be for us as well. Prayer should be like eating, drinking, or sleeping. It is a necessary function in life. We should examine ourselves to see how our prayer lives are going.

What place does prayer take in your life? Is it a few words thrown out only when the situation gets tough? Or do you see prayer as the lifeline that it is, connecting you to the Father?

Daring

Joshua spared Rahab the prostitute, with her family and all who belonged to her, because she hid the men Joshua had sent as spies to Jericho—and she lives among the Israelites to this day.

JOSHUA 6:25 NIV

Are you familiar with the story of Rahab? The book of Joshua holds her story. Joshua had sent spies to Jericho, Rahab's hometown, to figure out a way to attack. The spies, however, didn't make it out of the city before guards were alerted to their presence. Rahab hid them and lied to the officials searching for them, protecting the spies. In exchange, she asked that she and her family be spared from the impending destruction of the city.

The author points out to us that not only was Rahab a Canaanite, but she was also a prostitute. However, God honored her daring faith, and she is one of just five women to be mentioned in the lineage of Jesus. Rahab had heard what the Israelites God had done for them, and she chose to serve him. It was a daring move on her part, turning from her entire culture and life to serve God. As women of God, we are often called to go against our upbringing, our culture, and our society to do what we know is right. Let's be like Rahab: flawed but bold in Christ.

What daring moves need to be made in your life?

Distinguished

The LORD of hosts is exalted in justice,
and the Holy God shows himself holy in righteousness.
ISAIAH 5:16 ESV

Our God is an awesome God like no other! That's a truth that we can proclaim. God is set apart from all the other false gods and religions of this world. He is the only one that is perfectly holy in all his ways. He cannot be compared to created things because he is the Creator. The many attributes of God, as described in the Bible, set him apart from anything or anyone else that might try to exalt themselves.

Another notable thing that sets Christianity apart is the grace of God. The grace of God is exclusive to Christianity. All other religions have some sort of merit-based system or way that you work for the favor of God. Thanks to the Spirit, we know better. The one true God sent his Son to die for us. There is no way we could earn it on our own; it's a gift that we don't deserve. The grace of God stands out amongst all other religions because it is God reaching down toward humanity.

How can you reach back and accept this gift?

Enraptured

*"You have made known to me the paths of life;
you will fill me with joy in your presence."*
ACTS 2:28 NIV

This portion of Scripture comes after the disciples have been filled with the Holy Spirit. Peter is preaching, and he quotes the book of Psalms, specifically 16:11 here. In the psalm, David speaks lovingly of the Lord. Now, have you ever been in love? There is a difference between being in love and just loving someone. "In love" describes joy. You can tell if someone is in love by their actions and their focus. It seems like a magnet draws two people in love together. Their focus is completely upon one another.

David and Peter are talking about being in love with God. The relationship is defined by their focus being on God. Think about a wedding of two people in love. Their smiles and joy are deep and contagious to all their guests. Dear sister, you may feel like the embers of being in love with God have died for you, but he is still enraptured with you. Spend time in his presence, with no other goal but to be with the lover of your soul.

Would you define your relationship with God as being enraptured by him?

Faith

Overhearing what they said, Jesus told him,
"Don't be afraid; just believe."
MARK 5:36 NIV

Doubt is not the opposite of faith; fear is. This can be difficult to remember during hard times. Fear can manifest itself in our lives in many ways. When we get on the treadmill of worry, we give in to fear. When we try desperately to grasp for control, we let fear have that control. Many times in his ministry, Jesus tells people to not be afraid, to not worry, and to have faith.

What does worry do? What does it accomplish? Deep down, we all know that it accomplishes nothing. Faith turns our worries into prayers, entrusting those worries to the one who can do something about them. Anxiety may look like frantically searching for answers, finding a different area you can control and hyper-focusing on that, or lashing out in relationships. The disciples felt out of control several times in their time with Jesus. Think about the stories of the thousands who needed to be fed, or the giant waves that plummeted their boats. Jesus didn't ask them to take control of the situation. He just asked that they have faith in him.

When fear arises, do you swing toward worry or anxiety? What can you do to replace those with faith?

Deliverance

You are my hiding place;
You shall preserve me from trouble;
You shall surround me with songs of deliverance.

PSALM 32:7 NKJV

There are terms in the Bible that have multifaceted meanings. Deliverance is one of those. It can mean one thing or more than five things. The first is forgiveness of our sins. Second is physical health being restored, and third is freedom from spiritual bondage. The fourth refers to freedom from eternal death, and lastly, it can simply mean rescue from hard situations. What a wide variety of freedom is available to us!

The psalmist refers to songs of deliverance. There are many instances in Scripture when songs were used for freedom. David sang to King Saul, and it soothed his soul. Paul and Silas sang in prison, and they were freed. These instances put into practice songs of deliverance. So, what kind of deliverance do you need? The beauty of this psalm is that God promises to shelter us and keep us when trouble arises. Not only that, but we can also be surrounded by songs of victory over our situation. Victory, deliverance, freedom—these are God's melodies. Do you need deliverance today? Lift up your song.

What definition of deliverance are you looking for today?

Awesome

"O Lord God of heaven, the great and awesome God who keeps covenant and steadfast love with those who love him and keep his commandments."

NEHEMIAH 1:5 NRSV

Use a toy too much, and it eventually breaks. Use a word like *awesome* too much, and it loses its power. We've overused *awesome*, making it refer to everything from ice cream to TV shows. While that's not necessarily a bad thing, it makes verses like this duller than the author was trying to convey.

When the Bible says that God is an awesome God, it means that he is extremely impressive. He should invoke great admiration or daunting awe in you. Anytime someone approaches God in the Bible, you see this. They fall on their faces. They can't speak. Isaiah cried, "Woe to me, for I am unclean." They didn't do this to put on a show; they did this because there is no other response when face-to-face with our awesome, living, powerful God. This is a good place for us to be. In humility, on our knees before God, our posture shows that we remember who he is and who we are. He is the one true God. He is in control, not us. Let's bring awesome back, in reverent worship of the one who truly is.

How can you praise God today in awe?

Authentic

Love must be sincere.
Hate what is evil; cling to what is good.

ROMANS 12:9 NIV

Many of us gather our ideas of love from TV, books, and popular music while growing up. The atmosphere of our childhood homes also plays a large role. Though some good ideas may have been present, many of us grew up with a skewed view of love. Popular culture taught us things, our home life taught us things, but what does the Bible say true love is?

The go-to passage for knowing what genuine love should look like is 1 Corinthians 13. We need to align what we were taught, consciously or subconsciously, with what Scripture says love is. It can be surprising to see the stark contrast between the fabricated, fake version of the world's love and the authentic love of the one who is love himself. We are called to not only demonstrate that love to others, but also to accept that love for ourselves. God loves you as a father. Is that hard for you to grasp because of your upbringing? Jesus loves you like a friend, a sister. Have you been betrayed by friends and don't know what that should look like? Prayer and counseling can help us sort through authentic versus fake love, coming out on the other side stronger and able to love others well.

What skewed views of love might be hindering you from giving or receiving love?

Capable

Jesus looked at them and said,
"With man this is impossible,
but with God all things are possible."

MATTHEW 19:26 NIV

You are not capable of doing it. How's that for a pep talk? It should inspire you deeply. With the knowledge of not being able, the reality that is Christ arises. Without God, life is nothing more than a large series of obstacles. But with God, he lifts you above these obstacles and makes a way for you to fulfill his will.

We must recognize our inability to access the endless ability of God. Without Christ, you are incapable of loving your people well. But with Christ, who is love, you can love abundantly. Without God, you can't calm the storm around you or move the mountain in front of you. But with God, storms are calmed, seas are parted, and mountains are moved. You cannot heal or save anyone. But with the power of the Holy Spirit, people are saved. Healing comes. Freedom begins. Let us be women whose lives are dependent on the living God, seeking his power and strength to do the immeasurable that he promises to do through us.

What are you capable of doing in Christ?

Bountiful

"Remain in me, as I also remain in you.
No branch can bear fruit by itself;
it must remain in the vine.
Neither can you bear fruit unless you remain in me."
JOHN 15:4 NIV

Is there a farmers' market where you live? Farmers markets can be so fun, even to just stroll through on a sunny summer morning. The colors of abundant fruits, vegetables, and flowers make for a delightful array. Handcrafted goods, yummy baked treats, skilled musicians—what a celebration of the bounty of harvest time!

This is the picture that comes to mind when Jesus talks about believers bearing good fruit. We can be bountiful in good fruit or in bad, and the quality of our fruit depends on what (or who) we are connected to. We must abide deeply in Christ to have a bounty of good fruit in our lives. What does it mean to remain in Christ? If you have a fruit-bearing tree, and you cut off one of the branches and bring it inside, is it going to continue to bear fruit? What if you stick the branch into a pot of soil? It's not going to work. The branch needs to remain connected to bear fruit. Likewise, we must not try to abide in the world or attach ourselves to other life sources. Jesus is our source, and with him, our harvest will be bountiful.

How are you abiding in Christ right now?

April

✝

The LORD is my strength and my song;
he has given me victory.
This is my God, and I will praise him—
my father's God, and I will exalt him.

EXODUS 15:2 NLT

Aware

My soul waits in hope for the LORD
More than the watchmen for the morning;
Yes, more than the watchmen for the morning.

PSALM 130:6 NASB

There is more to our world than what meets the eye. What you can see around you is the physical realm. There is also the spiritual realm. We walk around unaware of the spiritual realm, unaware of things that are happening around us. In reading the Bible, however, we see that it is very active. We know that there are evil forces, along with God and his angels. To be aware of the spiritual realm is important because there is often more going on than our physical eyes can see.

That's why we must be diligent in prayer. In Scripture, we are told that Satan has been sent here to steal, kill, and destroy. He would like nothing more than to lead you away from Christ, to destroy your family, and to steal your witness. When you meet troubles, know that there can be other things going on. This is another reason why it is important to bring everything to God in prayer. Just like the watchmen kept watch overnight for the city, we must keep watch through prayer over our families.

How can you be more aware of the spiritual realm?

Belief

"Don't worry or surrender to your fear.
For you've believed in God,
now trust and believe in me also."

JOHN 14:1 TPT

When you get into your car to drive to work, you may flip on the radio and hear some news and the weather. Usually, most of the news is not in your area. A tornado hit a different part of the country, a bank was robbed, or a car accident happened in a different part of the city. Even though you didn't see them happen, you usually believe they did. You also believe the weather person when they say you might need an umbrella later.

We practice belief daily in different ways, but when it comes to belief in God, we often trip up. Fear or doubt creeps in stealthily when it comes to God. Why doesn't it when it comes to the news? It's because we have an enemy whose weapon of fear is used in any way possible to hinder us from belief. Faith is the one requirement of us in Scripture. It makes sense that our enemy would do whatever it takes to destroy that belief. If you are struggling in your belief of God, cry out to him. "Lord, I believe. Help my unbelief!" (Mark 9:24)

Can you identify where fear is hindering belief in your life?

Adopted

You have not received a spirit that makes you fearful slaves. Instead, you received God's Spirit when he adopted you as his own children. Now we call him, Abba, Father.

ROMANS 8:15 NLT

God did not pay the high cost of freedom for us to leave us as slaves to our fear and sin. He could have, but he did not. God takes our redemption a step further than we could have ever imagined and calls us his daughters. He could have redeemed us purely for service, for us to serve him as a harsh master. But that is not who he is. He is a kind, loving father. He pours his spirit into us to show us we are loved and accepted by him. What a beautiful blessing!

Using the word *Abba* in this context was extraordinary. No one in the culture at that time spoke of God in such an intimate, loving way. The only other person in the Bible who refers to God in this way is Jesus. He prays in this manner in the garden, crying out to God. God has given us the distinct privilege of speaking to him in the same manner. God is not your employer or your master, but rather your loving Father. Won't you turn to him in this manner today?

What does it mean to you that we have the privilege of calling God Abba?

Abundant

They feast on the abundance of your house;
you give them drink from your river of delights.
PSALM 36:8 NIV

Reading Psalm 36, you will see the phrases "your love," "your faithfulness," "your righteousness," and "your justice." The Psalmist uses large, grand metaphors when trying to convey these attributes of God. It boils down to the fact that God is endlessly abundant in his love, his faithfulness, his righteousness, and his justice. There is more than enough. They never run out.

We believers can get into a poverty mindset. This means that we don't approach God for something because we don't think there is enough, or we don't want to impose upon him. As though these attributes of his can run out! As if, since we needed him to be faithful before, we shouldn't ask again. That's not how the kingdom of God works. God is sufficient; there is more than enough. He does not hold back from his children or demand that you wait your turn. In fact, God desires that you draw from his strength, his mercy, and his abundance. He is a generous father, wanting all his children to be fulfilled.

How do you approach God?

Amiable

"May I find favor in your eyes, my lord," she said.
"You have put me at ease by speaking kindly
to your servant."

RUTH 2:13 NIV

A mother often says to her children, "How you speak to other people matters." It's a lesson that she hopes will carry into adulthood, and we should take to heart, too. It's about more than just being a polite member of society. As believers, we are ambassadors for Christ into our world. We are the ones that represent and show Christ to the lost world around us. Have you heard the phrase, "You might be the only Jesus they meet?" That's why how we speak and interact with people is important.

In this verse, Ruth is calmed and finds trust in Boaz because of the way he spoke to her. His kindness led to a story that is linked into the genealogy of Jesus. Imagine if Ruth had felt like she could not trust him. What if he had been harsh with her? You never know what kind of stories God wants to craft and doors he wants to open through our kindness. Every word we speak has an effect on someone's eternity. Let's pay attention to our tone and demeanor.

This passage is convicting. Is the Holy Spirit bringing anything to your mind?

Complete

The LORD will work out his plans for my life—
for your faithful love, O LORD, endures forever.
Don't abandon me, for you made me.

PSALM 138:8 NLT

Mozart, Michelangelo, Leonardo da Vinci. What do you think of when their names are mentioned? One is famous composer, two are a couple of the most famous artists in history. Perhaps some of their great music or paintings come to mind. Something all three of them have in common, however, is that each of them left unfinished work. Leonardo never finished his painting entitled "The Adoration of the Magi." Michelangelo never finished "The Entombment," and Mozart never finished his piece entitled "Requiem." What a shame! The world is missing out on beauty in these incomplete works.

Thankfully, our God does not leave things incomplete. He has promised to complete what he has started. God is the potter, shaping and molding the clay of your life. He is working, and he will not leave you, discard you, or forget about you. You are a masterpiece that he will complete. Praise God for this faithfulness and truth!

What good work has God started in you? How does his promise to be faithful bring you reassurance?

Dignified

God said, "Let us make man in our image, after our
likeness. And let them have dominion over the fish of
the sea and over the birds of the heavens and over the
livestock and over all the earth and over every creeping
thing that creeps on the earth."
GENESIS 1:26 ESV

Did your mother ever tell you to treat others the way you want
to be treated? Most of us want to be treated with dignity and
respect. Every single person is made in the image of God. There
is not one person who is a mistake or made to be below the
others. Every single person into whose eyes you look, Christ
died for them.

Our human pride fights to exalt ourselves. Pride and hate make
us look at another person's skin color and determine they are
less. It uses our words to make people feel less than, in person
or behind a screen. Our sinful natures would have us use and
discard other people for our own pleasure, pain management,
or to climb a ladder to success. We give our allegiance to our
country instead of our love to the people around us. Let us
repent of the many ways we have stripped our fellow human
beings of their dignity, remembering that Jesus showed dignity
and worth to everyone.

While you are repenting, what does God say you could do to
restore relationships?

Effective

*"This is to my Father's glory, that you bear much fruit,
showing yourselves to be my disciples."*

JOHN 15:8 NIV

We are all disciples of Christ. We want to bring Christ glory.
How can we know if we are effective disciples? Are the lives we
live truly bringing glory to the kingdom of God? Several times
in Scripture, Jesus speaks of our fruit. He tells us that apart
from him, we cannot bear fruit, and that those who abide in
him will bear good fruit. The answer to these questions is in
another question: what kind of fruit are you bearing? Are you
abiding in Christ? To abide means to dwell, for Christ to be
your home.

Dear sister, you do not need to try harder or strive longer to
produce good fruit. Good fruit comes naturally from the one who
is abiding in Christ. That's all you are asked to do. Just abide.
When was the last time you spent time with Jesus, simply existing
in his presence? Not looking for a way to improve, to learn your
next work assignment, or to find tips to share with those you
teach—just being. Abide with Jesus, and the fruit will come.

How can you make time to be in God's presence today?

Credited

*The words "it was credited to him" were written not
for him alone, but also for us, to whom God will credit
righteousness—for us who believe in him who raised Jesus
our Lord from the dead. He was delivered over to death for
our sins and was raised to life for our justification.*

ROMANS 4:23-24 NIV

Have you ever read a book that felt like it was written just
for you? Perhaps it was a grand fiction tale with such vivid
characters that you can see yourself in one of them. Maybe
it was a memoir written by a person whose experience is so
familiar, it could be your own. Paul is telling us that something
that was written long ago about Abraham's life was not just for
him. It was written for you!

You can put yourself into this story. The abundant credit of
righteousness that Abraham received as a result of his faith is
for you, too. If you have confessed Christ as Lord and believe
in his resurrection and your subsequent justification, then the
righteousness of God is yours. It covers you. When God looks
at you, he sees the righteousness of Christ. No longer does he
see a sinful woman. The payment has been made, and your
debt is credited in full. The balance doesn't just rest at zero. You
are given infinitely more because his righteousness is that rich.
Praise God that we find ourselves in such a story!

How can you express joy over the credit you have received?

Convinced

*I am convinced that nothing can ever separate us from
God's love. Neither death nor life, neither angels nor
demons, neither our fears for today nor our worries
about tomorrow--not even the powers of hell can separate
us from God's love.*

ROMANS 8:38-39 NLT

Paul stands convinced. He had processed everything and
decided that this is his final stance. The whole book of Romans
reads like a letter of persuasive evidence, and these verses are
the conclusive truth that Paul wants his readers to remember.
There is nothing that can pull or push us away or block us from
God's love. His love for us is more powerful than death, longer
lasting than life. No creature in heaven or hell can convince
God to take another course of action or to abandon his love
toward us. No fear you conjure will thwart him. God's love is
for you, end of story.

Many of us have been rejected or abandoned at some point in
our lives. It could have been by parents, friends, or a partner.
Though humans will unfortunately reject and hurt one another
frequently, God never will. It's an absolute truth that you can
bet on. In prayer, let us ask God to convince our wounded
hearts that his love for us is unending, as much as Paul is
convinced here.

*What feels like it is separating you from God? What truth can you
apply to that lie today?*

Rational

Paul said, "I am not out of my mind, most excellent Festus, but I am speaking true and rational words."
ACTS 26:25 ESV

Reading the entire chapter of Acts 26, you will find the context for our verse is that Paul had already been in prison for two years. After those two years, there was some turnover amongst the government, and Paul was brought before Festus. King Agrippa the Second was visiting and heard Paul's testimony. Paul stood up and gave his testimony, speaking of Jesus' resurrection and his conversion. This was when he was accused of being crazy. Interestingly enough, both men later decide that Paul isn't guilty of anything; he could have been set free. But Paul used the opportunity of being in chains to speak about the saving power of Jesus any chance he got.

When it comes to Jesus, Festus is a little bit right. We can't just let Jesus be a good prophet or a man who walked the earth. As C.S. Lewis wrote, if we hold to all the historical accounts that tell us Jesus was real, he must be one of three things: a dirty liar, a crazy man, or the Son of God. There are no other options. Paul, and many like him, were willing to be chained because they knew the truth. Jesus is the Son of God.

What do you hold as true about Jesus?

Proficient

Let every skillful craftsman among you
come and make all that the LORD has commanded.

EXODUS 35:10 ESV

In this verse, Moses is speaking to the people about building the tabernacle of God. He had been given specific instructions on how it was to look. Do you think that Moses could have built such an intricate building all by himself? He would have needed to be skilled in things like weaving, carpentry, smithing, and more. While that would make for an impressive resume, Moses was not that talented of a man! It took the entire community and their skills to make the temple.

You have skills and gifts that have been given to you by God. They may seem obscure to you, like weaving or glassblowing or solving equations. You may not know how God could ever use that skill for his glory. His plans are so much higher than ours, and he wastes nothing. He has a plan for your skills, and they are needed in the world and in the church body. It's up to us to practice those skills and be ready when God calls us to use them.

What skills do you have?

Receptive

*"Blessed are your eyes, because they see; and your ears,
because they hear. For truly I say to you that many
prophets and righteous men desired to see what you see,
and did not see it, and to hear what you hear,
and did not hear it."*

MATTHEW 13:16-17 ESV

Jesus often taught in parables. A parable is a simple story that illustrates the deeper moral or point that the teller is trying to make. He wasn't trying to be secretive or to make the gospel harder to access. He was making it available to those who had hearts to hear it.

Have you ever listened to a kid's audiobook or read a book out loud to a child? You might zone out and not really hear the story. How many times can one person read *Goodnight Moon* without zoning out? But the child eats it up because their heart is receptive and open to the story. Some people understood the parables. Some people thought they were too good to listen to such trivial stories and decided that Jesus was wasting their time. Elsewhere in Scripture, Jesus tells us to be like little children. When it comes to hearing a part of the Bible that maybe you've heard a thousand times, let us ask God to give us receptive ears to hear his Word and fresh eyes to see timeless truths.

What distracts you or keeps you from receiving the Word of God?

Servant

*You were called to freedom, brothers. Only do not use
your freedom as an opportunity for the flesh, but through
love serve one another. For the whole law is fulfilled in
one word: "You shall love your neighbor as yourself."*

GALATIANS 5:13-14 ESV

After a long day cooped up inside, the dogs burst out into the
yard with wild abandon. They race around in circles, jumping
and panting. Occasionally, they try to go past the underground
fence in the yard. Every single time, they get reeled back in.
Just because they are set free from their house to be in the
yard doesn't mean that all their boundaries have been erased.
Without the yard's boundaries, they could get in fights with
other dogs, be picked up by the cops, or run into a whole host
of other issues. The owner knows what is best for them by
keeping their boundaries in place.

Similarly, just because we are free from our sins in Christ
does not mean that all boundaries have been removed. Our
freedom should be lived out in such a way that we are honoring
and loving others. Who has God placed around you to love?
Servanthood must be carried out in community. Look at
your church body. How can you love others? Look in your
neighborhood. Who needs some encouragement? Let us show
love to the community around us by serving one another in love.

Where do you serve right now?

Saved

If you declare with your mouth, "Jesus is Lord," and believe in your heart that God raised him from the dead, you will be saved.

ROMANS 10:9 NIV

Use a word too much and it begins to lose meaning. Take the word *great*, for example. We use it to describe everything from our breakfast to a football game. We've used it so much that it's lost the punch that it should deliver. The word *saved* in the realm of Christianity can suffer the same fate. We hear pastors preach about being saved. We read the word in books and hear it everywhere. But what does being saved really mean? Being saved is not a get out of hell free card. It's not a prayer you pray once and go on your merry way.

Words can also be used in different ways. Not very instance of saved in the Bible references salvation. Take 1 Timothy 2:15, for example. Paul is not saying women's eternal future comes from having babies! Another translation for *saved* is "deliverance." In the Bible, we are presented with different scenarios of deliverance. Here in Romans, Paul is speaking of deliverance from sins. The gospel is simple, and powerful. Let us not let words lose their meaning by misunderstanding or misuse.

If you are a believer, what does it mean to you that you are saved?

Satisfied

Jesus said to them, "I am the bread of life;
whoever comes to me shall not hunger,
and whoever believes in me shall never thirst."

JOHN 6:35 ESV

Every person in the world wants to know what will make them happy. There are books written about it, conferences and seminars on it, and we all often go on the quest to find our happiness. From our childhood, we look for things that will bring us pleasure. We long for things that will bring us accomplishment, people who will make us feel a certain way. The problem with this is that we become like black holes, sucking in all that we desire and still wanting more.

God, the Creator of black holes, is the only one who can satisfy us. Pursuits are endless unless they end in Christ. When we find our satisfaction in Christ, we bring him glory, we find contentment, and it is in our best interest. Becoming a believer, however, doesn't flip a switch and make us satisfied. It's a continuous, working relationship of us seeking the Lord and him responding to our needs. If you feel dissatisfied, don't be discouraged. Turn to the Lord and ask him to fill you again.

In what other areas do you seek satisfaction apart from Christ?

Redemption

In him we have redemption through his blood,
the forgiveness of sins, in accordance with
the riches of God's grace.

EPHESIANS 1:7 ESV

Jesus spoke seven phrases on the cross. "It is finished" is one of the seven. In Greek, the phrase is a single word: *tetelestai*. Many have viewed the statement as a phrase about letting go, a phrase of release. However, it is more of a victory cry. This phrase has been found on receipts form the time to indicate that the person paid in full.

When criminals were put into prison, they were given a slip of paper with their crimes written on it, and it was nailed to the door above their cell. It was called a certificate of debt. It stayed nailed above so all could make sure that the full debt was paid. When the criminal had served the full sentence, *tetelestai* was stamped onto their paper. Imagine the recognition when those who watched Jesus die heard him say this phrase. This victory cry tells us that the debt has been paid, and it has been paid in full. Praise God for this victory he has won for us!

What does this deeper understanding of the phrase Jesus spoke mean to you?

Vitality

*He made from one man every nation of mankind to live
on all the face of the earth, having determined allotted
periods and the boundaries of their dwelling place, that
they should seek God, and perhaps feel their way toward
him and find him. Yet he is actually not far from each
one of us. "In him we live and move and have our being."*

ACTS 17:26-28 NIV

God is present in all his creation, yet he remains distinct from
it. This is not saying that the sun is God or the moon or any
specific element of nature. It pushes back against those who
think God is distant, those who think that he created us,
dropped us here, and left it all to play out by chance. No, God is
near, and those three words should bring immense comfort to
the believer. He is the vitality of all that is around us. Our very
breath is a gift from him. Our placement on earth is determined
by him. His words make the sun rise and set, the snow blow
and the rain fall.

We often hear that our world, including ourselves, is corrupted
by sin. While sin and the fall did affect all of creation, it did not
remove the presence of God from it. It could not banish him to
some remote corner of the universe or displace him from our lives.
In fact, God has done the opposite and has overcome all of that.
He is very near to us. Let his presence soothe your soul today.

Do you recognize how God is near?

Trust

*Commit your way to the LORD
trust in him, and he will act.*
PSALM 37:5 ESV

When life gets hard, what do your prayers sound like? Some tend to make bargains with God. "If you'll just give me this, God, I'll do anything." Other prayers are full of panic. We demand of God to relinquish to us what we want. God feels so far from us, as though we must beg and plead him to listen. Let us learn to use this example from Psalms. This short verse teaches us to commit and surrender.

To commit your plans to the Lord means to involve him in the planning process. It means trusting the core character traits about him, like his goodness, and believing what his Word says about him working things together for our good. We believe he will act on our behalf, even if it doesn't look like we want it to. To surrender means to let go, to acknowledge that God's ways are higher than ours and to, again, trust in his goodness. Acknowledging his character in this way instead of demanding our own way reminds our souls that God is near. Instead of trying to quiet our fears by grasping for control, let us commit and surrender our fears to God.

What are you entrusting to God today?

Unshakable

Cast your cares on the LORD and he will sustain you;
he will never let the righteous be shaken.
PSALM 55:22 NIV

There is a misconception about ballerinas. You might think that they are light as feather, graceful and delicate, and that you could push them over with the slightest touch. The reality is, though they look that way, they are incredibly strong. A good ballerina pulls strength from her core and is unmovable, even when pushed. There is a quiet strength about them as they use muscles that most of us don't even know we have.

Dear sister, to be unshakable in a tempestuous world, our relationship with Christ needs to be our core. The center of our beings holds us up and makes us move. This is the sustaining power that David is talking about. Just like ballerinas, this is where our strength comes from. Being full of grace and meekness does not mean being weak. Quite the opposite! It means being incredibly strong because your strength comes from the Lord. He will sustain you. He will make you unshakable.

What cares do you need to give to the Lord?

Wholesome

A wholesome tongue is a tree of life,
But perverseness in it breaks the spirit.

PROVERBS 15:4 NKJV

Have you ever gone on a health kick? Maybe you are the person amongst your friends that is known as the health guru. When people think of their health, most focus purely on the physical. While we need to pursue health for our bodies, it's important to not neglect other areas, like emotional and spiritual health.

The Bible says that God cares about our hearts; that is, who we really are. We can be physically healthy and inwardly rotting away. Today's verse from Proverbs talks about what comes out of your mouth. Is it wholesome? Elsewhere is Scripture, we are told that out of the overflow of the heart, our mouths speak. What an excellent indicator for our inward health! We have immense power when we speak of bringing healing through the power of the Holy Spirit to the souls of others. Our words can also crush people. What we say matters. Are you kind with your words? Do you hold your tongue when needed? Do you share the truth of the gospel? Do you pray with others? Do you use your words to stand up for justice when the time arises?

Ask yourself these questions to do a checkup on the health of your heart.

Unashamed

*I am not ashamed of the gospel, because it is the power
of God that brings salvation to everyone who believes:
first to the Jew, then to the Gentile.*

ROMANS 1:16 ESV

Many of us live in a part of society that is saturated with
Bibles and Christian teaching. It may seem unfamiliar and
odd, then, to think of being ashamed of the gospel. Paul
explains elsewhere in Scripture that for the Jews, the gospel is
scandalous and offensive. The fact that the Messiah would die,
and the way that he died, was offensive. In Deuteronomy, it
says that anyone who is hung on a tree is cursed. The Gentiles,
Paul explained, think that the gospel message is foolishness
because it is irrational to them. Their intellect tells them that
the message is foolish.

But Paul does not care; he is unashamed in the face of both.
Paul knows the power of God. He knows what he has been
freed from. The thoughts of the entire society around him are
of no concern to him even when they try to kill him for it, reject
him for it, and ruin his reputation for it. The cost of the gospel
is high for some, but it cost Christ the most.

Have you counted the cost?

Teachable

Whoever ignores instruction despises himself,
but he who listens to reproof gains intelligence.
PROVERBS 15:32 ESV

When looking for a spouse, some of the top character qualities that people look for are confidence, generosity, honesty, humor, and loyalty. These are all excellent qualities. We should also add teachable to the list. What does it mean to be teachable? It means that you are willing to learn. There is a large degree of humility that comes into play for this quality as well. To learn, you must be able to admit you don't know everything.

A teachable person does not live in an echo chamber, listening to the thoughts and ideas of only those they agree with. They listen to others' stories, consider their points of view, and humbly admit they could be wrong while holding fast to truth. We are all finite beings with limited understanding. God says he will give us wisdom whenever we ask, and sometimes that wisdom can come from a fellow human being. Jesus was the ultimate example of humility and teachability. He was constantly consulting the Father and displayed a great ability to listen to others. Let us prize this quality and strive to be like Christ.

Would you consider yourself teachable?

Resolute

I have fought the good fight,
I have finished the race,
I have kept the faith.

2 TIMOTHY 4:7 NCV

You have probably heard the hymn "I Have Decided to Follow Jesus." This hymn, written in India, holds a line that says, "No turning back, no turning back." The author is conveying a resolute decision to follow Christ, no matter the cost. In today's verse, Paul writes that he has finished his race. One does not easily finish a race. It takes determination; it takes being resolute. To get to the end of our lives and hear Christ say, "Well done, good and faithful servant," we must be resolute.

What does this look like in practice? It means stepping out in faith when we get the nudge. It means taking God at his word and believing, no matter what is thrown our way. It means holding fast to the truth and listening to the Holy Spirit. The journey of a Christian is not an easy one. Many things that are thrown at you will test your faith. The key is to keep turning back to God, never away. Turn toward God, and he who is faithful will keep you faithful till the end.

Do you desire to hear those words from Christ at the end of your race?

Reconciliation

God has made all things new,
and reconciled us to himself,
and given us the ministry of reconciling others to God.

2 CORINTHIANS 5:18 TPT

Do you know the parable of the prodigal son? There are three main characters in the story: the wayward son, the son who stayed home, and the father. Many of us find we identify most with one character. In reality, we are each of these at different points in our lives. We are the wayward son, desperately in need of reconciliation with God. This is not a move on our part toward God, but God's move toward us. His desire is for us to be reconciled to him. At times, we become the older brother. We have resentments or judgments about others, and we don't want to forgive or listen to them. We forget that we have been forgiven much and should forgive much.

Hopefully, as we grow in our faith, we will be most like the father, our heavenly Father, who wants all his children to be reconciled to him. We should look at every human being as someone who needs to be reconciled to God and not shy away from proclaiming the gospel to them. The ministry of reconciliation is the spreading of the gospel, and God has entrusted you with it.

What are you going to do with this responsibility?

Promises

He has granted to us his precious and very great
promises, so that through them you may become
partakers of the divine nature, having escaped from the
corruption that is in the world because of sinful desire.

2 PETER 1:4 ESV

Do you like to hunt for treasure? Treasure hunting is a fun hobby, and for some, a profession. You might see people with their metal detectors out on the beach for hours, searching for something that they don't even know is there. The thrill of the finds, even if they are few and far between, keeps them going.

Do you know what Scripture is full of? The promises of God. Like the treasure hunters on TV or at the beach, Christians should spend daily time searching out the promises of God. They are more precious than fine gems, worth more than anything you could find hidden in the countryside. Even better, they aren't trying to hide from us! The Bible is full of these precious promises, glimmering jewels just waiting to be found. God's magnificent promises exceed anything we could face in our lives. Let us be treasure hunters, daily picking up the Word of God, seeking out his promises, and rejoicing in them.

What promise of God is your treasure today?

Modest

Women should adorn themselves in respectable apparel, with modesty and self-control, not with braided hair and gold or pearls or costly attire.

1 TIMOTHY 2:9 ESV

Can you think of a more abused word in church culture today than *modesty*? This word, used in 1 Timothy, has been used to shame women over the way they dress. The Greek word for modest used here is *kosmios*, which translates as "respectable." This same word is used in the very next chapter to describe how men should behave as well. Modesty is not just an issue for women, as we may have been led to believe. Paul wrote a very specific letter to his mentee, Timothy. He addressed several groups of people in the letter regarding their behavior, one of which happened to be the women.

This verse is asking where your identity lies. It is not what store you shop at or how much clothing you can cover yourself with. The women he wrote to had a propensity to find their value in their appearance, to gain status through fine things and flaunt it as such. The encouragement is for humility. Who are we to boast in, as Paul tells us elsewhere in Scripture? We are to boast in Christ alone and display humility as our Savior did. That is what true modesty looks like: a man or a woman clothed the humility of Jesus.

What negative connotations does this verse carry for you? Does today's explanation help you find a better understanding?

Intimacy

As for me, how good it is to be near God!
PSALM 73: 28 NLT

Have you ever been in a large crowd but felt alone? It's a common occurrence. Spatial proximity to other humans does not guarantee intimacy with them. Consider knowledge. You can study about the Queen of England for months and learn a lot, but do you really know her? No. Knowledge does not guarantee intimacy. What about finding the right setting? Say a husband lights candles, makes a delicious dinner, and fills the room with flowers. A surefire way to gain intimacy? Wrong. Though the aesthetic of the room might be wonderful, the hearts of the couple can still be distant.

As believers, we often make these same mistakes when seeking intimacy with God. Intimacy in a relationship requires trust. There are many ways you can try to build intimacy, but trust is foundational. The non-secret to being intimate with God is trust, or belief. It's all he requires of us. We trust that he has redeemed us, but trust goes beyond that as well. If you feel distant from God, examine the trust between you. Have you been disappointed by God recently? Has sin disrupted your relationship? Have you pulled back in self-protection?

Ask yourself these self-examining questions to help clear a path for greater intimacy with God.

Honor

*Love each other with genuine affection
and take delight in honoring each other.*
ROMANS 12:10 NLT

Many western churches recognize Pastor Appreciation
Month and make an effort to honor their pastors in October.
Throughout the year, some churches might hold special
events for their volunteers as a way to say thank you. Flowers
and small trinkets are given out on days like Mother's Day
and Father's Day to honor those respective people in the
congregation. These are all ideas that try to implement what
Paul is writing to the Roman church. The "each other" he refers
to specifically addresses those within the body of Christ.

How can the body of Christ outdo itself and take delight in
honoring one another? This is not an exhortation for only
church staff. This is for you. How can you show your fellow
brothers and sisters in Christ that you value them? We can
acknowledge their accomplishments, repent of jealousy or envy,
show each person respect, refrain from gossip, and express
gratitude. These are ways mature believers can express honor
toward each other that don't cost a penny. An atmosphere of
delightful preference fosters a healthy church body.

What part can you play in honoring a fellow believer this week?

Heritage

We are surrounded by a great cloud of people whose lives tell us what faith means. So let us run the race that is before us and never give up.

HEBREWS 12:1 NCV

This verse comes to us right after what is known as the faith chapter. Take a minute to go back and read Hebrews 11. The faith chapter is story after story of men and women who chose to have faith in God against all circumstances. We read names like Abraham, David, Moses, and Rahab. There is even a section for people who remain nameless but whose faith did not go unseen.

Dive deep into their individual stories because this is our heritage. This is the legacy of the church. These are the men and women who went before you, and they are notable because they had faith. They believed that God would do what he said he would do, even when it seemed impossible. The list doesn't end in Hebrews. It stretches on throughout history to the present, and it includes many whose names we will never utter again, but their place in history is set as faithful servants of the one true God.

This is your legacy. What legacy will you leave?

May

"This is my command—be strong and courageous!
Do not be afraid or discouraged, For the LORD
your God is with you wherever you go."

JOSHUA 1:9 NLT

Friendly

Be kind to one another, tenderhearted,
forgiving one another,
as God in Christ forgave you.
EPHESIANS 4:32 ESV

Have you ever been the new kid? Most of us have at some point. Whether you were eighteen and starting college or thirty-eight and starting a new job, the experience is similar. It's hard to be the new kid. Everyone seems settled into their routines and relationships, and you are unsure of how you fit in. Think of your experience. Was there someone who was welcoming to you? Maybe you started at a new church and a member pushed past the awkward small talk and invited you over; they welcomed you. Maybe someone at the new job gave you some pointers. At school, perhaps another student welcomed you by showing you around.

To be welcomed is such a wonderful feeling. It's also a vital part of the great commission to welcome people with the kindness and love of Christ, from those in our neighborhoods to people in faraway countries. You have been welcomed into the family of God by the Trinity. Let us do likewise, showing a kind and welcoming spirit to those around us.

Who does God bring to mind that you can welcome with kindness?

Adoration

How right they are to adore you.

SONG OF SOLOMON 1:4 NLT

Have you heard the acronym ACTS? It stands for Adoration, Confession, Thanksgiving, and Supplication. It is one of many tools used to teach people to pray. When you remember ACTS, you cover four different parts of prayer. Confession is common in prayers and self-explanatory. Thanksgiving is popular as well, as even nonbelievers have been taught to give thanks around a dinner table. Supplication involves requests and presenting our needs before God. But what is adoration?

Adoration is important because it turns us toward the character of God and his Word. When we lift our gaze in adoration, it brings perspective to our lives, making God our center and his love the softening agent in our hard places. When we adore, we fall in love with God again. We can recognize lies we have believed about who he is and squash them with truth. Let us familiarize ourselves with this aspect of prayer, no longer skipping ahead to the parts that are about us. but taking time to focus on who he is.

What characteristic of God can you adore him for today?

Appreciated

We give thanks to God always for all of you,
constantly mentioning you in our prayers.

1 THESSALONIANS 1:2 ESV

You can tell a lot about what a person values by what they appreciate. In his many letters, Paul opens all but two with thanksgiving for the believers. Paul and his co-workers valued the body of Christ scattered around the region and noticed God at work in their lives. How encouraging it must have been for those believers to hear that Paul prayed for them and gave thanks to God for them.

We are prone to hold these kinds of ideas inside. Instead, let's follow the example of Paul and share some appreciation. What an encouragement you could be to a fellow brother or sister in Christ! Appreciation lets us know we are not alone and not unseen, and it is good for the soul. So, let's appreciate people. Say thank you. Pray for them. Send them a note, a text, or a phone call. Acknowledge the progress they have made, and the way God is working in their lives. Don't let it just be an unspoken thought; give it power by communicating it.

Who comes to mind when you think of giving appreciation?
Contact that person today!

Brave

The wicked flee when no one pursues,
but the righteous are as bold as a lion.

PROVERBS 28:1 NRSV

Satan is known as the accuser. He often brings up our sin, our fallen nature, and our shortcomings. Our own minds rally against us, reminding us of all the times we have failed and fallen short. These accusations can be crippling, but they don't have to be. We can be brave in the face of our accusations and guilt because we are righteous in Christ.

The beauty of the cross is that when God looks at us, he does not see our own righteousness, which is described in the Bible as filthy rags; rather, he sees Christ. Christ is righteous, perfect, and without sin. You are free from condemnation because you are in him. You can stand and boldly face those accusations because in Christ, you are righteous. When the lies come, when they flood our minds and try to remind us of who we have been or what we have done, stand bravely. Remind your inner accusers of the cross. Remind them of Christ. Remember that God sees you righteous in Christ, and nothing can change that.

Pray a brave prayer declaring your status in Christ. What has he set you free from?

Community

You will receive power when the Holy Spirit comes on you; and you will be my witnesses in Jerusalem, and in all Judea and Samaria, and to the ends of the earth.

ACTS 1.8 NIV

You, dear sister, are called by Christ to help fulfill the great commission. In this moment, you might think to yourself that isn't true. You may not feel called to move overseas or serve in full-time ministry, but the reality is that every single believer is asked to fulfill the great commission. A little further on in Acts, we are told that God placed each of us in our specific places and in this specific time for a purpose.

God has placed you in the community where you currently live to spread the good news of who he is. Jerusalem was the current community of the disciples; that was their home. Judea was the region, and Samaria was an even broader placement. Some of the disciples went far, taking the gospel to other countries, but some stayed right in Jerusalem. Near or far, they did not forget that they had the responsibility to share the gospel with their community. Are you merely a resident of your current neighborhood, or do you make an impact?

What communities might God be asking you to bring his good news into?

Brilliant

The Lord God is brighter than the brilliance of a sunrise!
Wrapping himself around me like a shield,
he is so generous with his gifts of grace and glory.
Those who walk along his paths with integrity
will never lack one thing they need, for he provides it all!

PSALM 84:11 TPT

Close your eyes and think of the most beautiful sunrise you have ever seen. They start slow, with the darkness of the witching hour still laying low around the land. Sometimes, you blink and realize that more light has been added. From deep blues, streaks of pink and orange form, light slowly cascading across the tops of the trees. And then, the sun peaks over the horizon, brilliant and warm, bathing the world in new light.

If you've been in a dark season, let that image lead you from the creation of a sunrise to the brilliance of our Creator. Let the warmth and brilliance of Jesus Christ envelop you. Find safety in the light of his embrace. Sometimes, we don't need more knowledge, deeper prayers, or harder acts of service. We don't need a big worship service or impressive preaching; we just need to sit with Jesus and enjoy the sunrise.

Spend extra time in meditative prayer. Focus on Jesus as the light that reaches into the darkest parts of you.

Benevolent

When you, a mere human being, pass judgment on them and yet do the same things, do you think you will escape God's judgment? Or do you show contempt for the riches of his kindness, forbearance and patience, not realizing that God's kindness is intended to lead you to repentance?

ROMANS 2:3-4 NIV

Do you know what the Latin word *omni* means? It means all. In the Bible, God is not just described as benevolent, which means good or kind, but he is "omnibenevolent," or all good. This means that he is all good. Any action, motive, thought, or response from him is all good, always.

We see this play out in Romans as Paul preaches about God's kindness. His kindness is what leads us to repentance. Isn't that interesting? Many people might say that a guilty conscience or an inner good is what draws them to confess their wrongdoings. But it is truly the kindness of God that brings us to the place of repentance. In his goodness, he wants goodness for us. His plan and his ways are good, and when we sin, we go against those. His amazing love for us runs so deeply and richly that he will not leave us in our sinful mess. Instead, he gently leads us to goodness by forgiving us.

How do you see God's goodness displayed in your life?

Ability

Then Moses said to the LORD, "Please, LORD, I have never been eloquent, neither recently nor in time past, nor since you have spoken to your servant; for I am slow of speech and slow of tongue." The LORD said to him, "Who has made man's mouth? Or who makes him mute or deaf, or seeing or blind? Is it not I, the LORD? Now then go, and I, even I, will be with your mouth, and teach you what you are to say."

EXODUS 4:10-12 NIV

This exchange between Moses and God comes to us many years after Moses had murdered a man and fled into the wilderness. While tending some sheep, he encounters the burning bush, a story familiar to many of us. God appears to him in the burning bush and tells him to go back to the Egyptian pharaoh and demand the release of God's people. God laid out the whole plan for him, and Moses responded with fearful doubts about his own ability.

You might relate to Moses; we all do at some point. We see what God is calling us to do, and then we look in the mirror and wonder, "How, Lord?" Maybe you don't think you have the financial resources, or you don't see the gifts that God has given you, or you have some physical ailment that you think disqualifies you. Whatever our doubts, is it not the Lord who gives us the strength and abilities to carry out the tasks he has for us? God has great plans for you. All he needs is a willing heart.

What doubts are keeping you from stepping out in faith?

Connected

From him the whole body, joined and held together by every supporting ligament, grows and builds itself up in love, as each part does its work.

EPHESIANS 4:16 NIV

Consider the human body. It is mind-blowing how God made our bodies! So many different parts, big and small, have to work together to keep you going every day. Each part, from the cells to the skull, has a purpose and a function. This is how the body of Christ should function as well.

Think of a baby. Studies suggest that babies who are isolated are far more prone to disease and a failure to thrive. We Christians cannot live in isolation. We need the rest of the body, and we have gifts that the rest of the body needs, too. We must value and protect unity within the body of Christ. It's notable that Paul mentions love because unity is impossible without love. We must grow in love for each other and for Christ, who is the head. Let us treat church like a body and connect with all its parts.

Do you regularly minster to and receive from your fellow brothers and sisters, or is church an obligation to you?

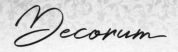

*At the name of Jesus every knee should bow, of those in
heaven, and of those on earth, and of those under the
earth, and that every tongue should confess that Jesus
Christ is Lord, to the glory of God the Father.*

PHILIPPIANS 2:10-11 NKJV

Are you a history buff? It can be fascinating to glimpse the past
through shows or books, seeing how people lived and what was
different. For example, previous periods in history had more
monarchies than we do today. The rules about what to do or
not do around royals can be extensive. Even in modern-day
England, there are certain ways to greet, sit, and converse with
the queen or king of the era.

In the Bible, we are told that when Jesus returns, the rules
will be simple. Every knee will bow. Every tongue will confess.
There will be no wiggle room on it at that point. Jesus, King of
kings, will rule and reign forever. Right now, you have a choice
to either bow your knee to the King or continue in rebellion
against him. Our days on this earth, and our option to choose,
will not last forever. Let us make sure that our knees are bowed
to Jesus, our tongues confess him as Lord, and our allegiance
lies only with him.

Do you bow your knee to Jesus?

Consistent

Long ago you laid the foundation of the earth
and made the heavens with your hands.
They will perish, but you remain forever;
they will wear out like old clothing.
You will change them like a garment and discard them.
But you are always the same;
you will live forever.

PSALM 102:25-27 NIV

Sometimes when we read the Bible, we think the God of the Old Testament seems very different from the God of the New Testament. God of the Old Testament might seem harsh and angry. The God in the New Testament, revealed through Jesus, is pure love. But God is consistent, the same from the beginning of time until now. Even in the Old Testament, God constantly calls his people back to himself out of love.

In both Testaments, God is just in all his ways. His justice and mercy rest in perfect balance. The consistency of God is reassuring because we, and those we love, can be flaky. It's part of human nature. Not only can we be flaky, but we can also ride a roller coaster of emotions, change our minds to suit ourselves, and not be true to our word. Though we do all these things, God does not. Our God is a safe place, consistent and never changing.

What reassurance do you receive from God being consistent?

Decent

*Put on all of God's armor so that you will be able
to stand firm against all strategies of the devil.*

EPHESIANS 6:11 NLT

The definition of decent that we are focusing on today is
"suitable in words, behavior, dress, or ceremony." When you go
to the beach, what is suitable attire? Bathing suits, sundresses,
and sunglasses, of course! Growing up, did your parents ever
tell you to use your indoor voice? That's proper behavior for
a place. In the same way, God equips us to face our days by
giving us the proper dress. We will face spiritual warfare daily,
and because of this, we need to suit up.

Paul writes about several pieces of armor in Ephesians 6.
He talks about taking up the helmet of salvation. There is
the sword of the spirit, the belt of truth, the breastplate of
righteousness, your feet protected by the gospel of peace, and
lastly the shield of faith. Each piece of armor protects different
areas of your life and different areas that Satan likes to attack.
You would never go to a physical war without the suitable
offensive and defensive tools. Likewise, suit up for your day.
Dig deeper into each of these pieces of armor to see what God
has provided for you.

*Which part of the armor of God most appeals to your current
situation?*

Energetic

*Who gave himself for us to redeem us from all
lawlessness and to purify for himself a people for his own
possession who are zealous for good works.*

TITUS 2:14 ESV

What makes you feel full of energy? Give it some thought.
It has been said that our calling is where the world's needs
and our passions collide. When put in those terms, can you
answer better? We are all called to be energetic for good works,
but those good works are not carbon copies of one another.
God has gifted you in a specific manner, given you a unique
perspective and story, and placed you in this time in history for
a purpose. Don't brush off the things you are passionate about
as meaningless.

God created you the way you are, and he wants to use you to
bring glory to his kingdom. What happiness can be found
when your soul comes alive with serving God! Try to refrain
from looking at the church and only seeing the roles that stand
out: pastor, teacher, etc. It can be discouraging if you don't
fit into one of those molds. Instead, figure out what you are
talented at, what story God wants you to tell, and what people
God wants you to reach. Then, channel your energy into that.
To God be the glory!

What makes you feel full of energy?

Determined

*"Stand firm,
and you will win life."*
LUKE 21:19 NIV

Here is the new catchphrase for us all, short and sweet. Who wants to win at life? It feels good to win! You might think that someone was crazy if they told you that they knew the secret to winning at life. Life! That's a big game. Jesus knows the secret though, and he has won. He has conquered sin and death and secured victory. We all stand victorious in Christ.

The battle has been won, but it's not game over. Game over comes when Christ returns, and we enter the age to come. What a glorious day that will be! Until then, we must be determined to stand firm, remembering that Christ is victorious. We must remember that no weapon formed against us will prosper. No enemy has power over us. We are free, and we have been set free for good. You want to win at life? Stand firm on all the promises of God and shout out a victory cry today. He has won!

How can you stand firm today?

Equipped

May the God of peace who brought again from the dead
our Lord Jesus, the great shepherd of the sheep, by the
blood of the eternal covenant, equip you with everything
good that you may do his will, working in us that which
is pleasing in his sight, through Jesus Christ, to whom be
glory forever and ever. Amen.

HEBREWS 13:20-21 ESV

Imagine you are getting ready to bake a cake. Naturally, you walk upstairs into your office. You get out some paper, pens, a stapler. Maybe some glue, too. You mix them all together, and you get a mess! If you want to bake a cake, it doesn't make any sense to be in an office using office supplies, does it? You need to be in the kitchen with the proper equipment, like an oven, bowl, and spatula.

In the same way, God is going to call you to some radical things in your life: things like loving your enemy, telling others about the gospel, and displaying hospitality. No matter what God calls you to, he will equip you for it. To try and do it with our own strength with just our skills is like trying to bake a cake with office supplies. Asking God to equip us, and letting his Holy Spirit work through us, will be a pleasing aroma before the Lord.

What do you need God to equip you with today?

Fearless

Yahweh is my revelation-light,
and the source of my salvation.
I fear no one!
I'll never turn back and run, for you, Yahweh,
surround and protect me.
When evil ones come to destroy me,
they will be the ones who turn back.
My heart will not fear even if an army rises to attack.
I will not be shaken, even if war is imminent.

PSALM 27:1-3 TPT

As king, David had plenty of things to worry about and fear. He speaks often in Psalms about enemies, including here in Psalm 27:2. Can you relate? Maybe you feel like trouble has come and camped out in your front yard, never to leave. It could be a chronic illness, marriage problems, financial insecurity, out-of-control kids, or conflict with friends. Maybe you wonder if God even hears your desperate prayers.

David didn't have to run from his enemies; he had the perfect place to hide. When trouble camps out at our doors and shoots its fiery arrows into our lives, we don't need to hightail it out of there. We can fearlessly stand and face them because we are hidden in Christ. He is our refuge and safety, the one who surrounds and protects us. No matter what circumstance you face today, you can be bold and unafraid, because Yahweh protects you.

How do you feel God's loving protection in your life right now?

Graceful

She is clothed with strength and dignity,
and she laughs without fear of the future.
When she speaks, her words are wise,
and she gives instructions with kindness.

PROVERBS 31:25-26 NLT

Scripture often uses clothing to relate to a person's spiritual state. We see this in Genesis, with Adam and Eve in the garden, all the way to the book of Revelation speaking about believers clothed in white for purity. Though the Proverbs 31 woman, described in the above verses, has fine linen clothing, it is not the outer garments that make her a good example, but the spiritual ones she wears. She clothes herself in strength of character and gracefulness of conduct.

These things are not reserved for women. Men should clothe themselves in these things, too, for these are fruits of the Spirit. The Proverbs 31 woman is graceful, as in "full of grace," because the fruit of the Holy Spirit is in her life. She is a woman no different from you or me. She is an example because the Holy Spirit is displaying his character in her life. Let us be women who are full of grace toward those around us by living our lives in submission to the Holy Spirit and desiring for his fruits to grow.

What does it mean to you to be graceful?

Hope

Hope deferred makes the heart sick,
but a dream fulfilled is a tree of life.

Proverbs 13:12 NIV

What makes the heart sick? For many people it's grief, pain, loss, and hurt. Being sick is not fun! So how do you remedy this sickness when life inevitably gives you these things? They can seem impossible to escape, but the remedy is hope. Hope comes in many ways. Hope is a burning light in what seems like never-ending darkness. Hope is a shield to protect you from the blows of loss, an escape from the clutches of grief, a foundation in a sea of pain.

When we have no hope, we really don't know what to do with ourselves. Our whole lives are constructed by and around hope. Without hope, we would have nothing to look forward to, nothing to live for, and nothing to fight for. When Jesus died on the cross, he gave us a way. A way to conquer death, overcome sin, and be with him forever. That way is hope. Don't delay hope making your heart sick; choose hope and be a part of the tree of life.

Where does your hope lie?

Identity

If anyone is in Christ, he is a new creation.
The old has passed away; behold, the new has come.

1 CORINTHIANS 5:17 ESV

From a young age, people like to label other people. We put each other in groups at school: the cool kids, the band kids, the goth kids, and so on. We don't let go of this labeling obsession once we leave high school. Even as adults, we like to fit others into neat categorical boxes. Maybe some of these labels you impose on yourself. Perhaps they make you feel safe, or they are what you have been told your whole life. It might be pretty, plain, talented, rebellious, a bother, athletic, smart, nerdy, and on and on.

Perhaps it is time we shake off all these labels that we let define us and take on just one—in Christ. The Bible has a lot to say about who you are in Christ. You are chosen, loved, a child of God, a friend of God, justified...and this wonderful list goes on. You can do a simple internet search and find sheets holding the whole list of excellent verses on your identity in Christ. Don't let labels, good or bad, be the shaping factor in your life. Accept your identity in Christ and let your status as new creation reign.

What label do you need to shake off?

Kindness

"Love your enemies, and do good, and lend, expecting nothing in return, and your reward will be great, and you will be sons of the Most High, for he is kind to the ungrateful and the evil."

LUKE 6:35 ESV

Giving kindness to those who are kind to us is easy. When Jesus asks us to be kind to our enemies, that can be difficult. You might not think you have any enemies, but you don't need to declare war to place them in enemy camp. It might be that girl that you scroll past on social media, full of jealousy. Perhaps it's the lady at Bible study who seems to have all the right answers. Maybe a friend at book club said something hurtful and you never resolved it.

Satan wants nothing more than to tear your relationships to the ground and put deep roots of destructive bitterness into your heart. That's why Jesus tells us to love our enemies. Jesus sets the example for us. He loved his enemies; he loved us when we were still considered enemies of God. One way to start practicing kindness toward those you don't get along with is prayer. Say a prayer for them, or simply speak their name in prayer to Jesus if you can't find good words. Watch God work in your heart and in that relationship.

Who do you need to pray for today?

Important

"You shall love the LORD your God with all your heart and with all your soul and with all your mind and with all your strength."

MARK 12:30 ESV

What does it really mean to love God and to obey him? It is easy to swing like a pendulum. On one side, you have those who try to follow every rule to a T, making the Bible nothing more than an impossible rule book. On the other side, you have those that think their idea of free love is enough, and that since God has set them free, they can do whatever they please. The first way results in a dry religion that inevitably will lead to failure and guilt, and the second can weaken faith and hurt others.

Jesus combats both tendencies by presenting to a curious scribe the most important commandment. With all our being—our central hearts, our intelligent minds, our willpower—we are to love God. This pushes against legalism because it encourages relationships. It pushes against endless freedom, because we are to love others as we love ourselves and love God, which means we can't do whatever we please. The greatest commandment brings us balance. Praise Jesus for his wise words!

Do you tend to swing toward freedom or legalism? Why do you think that is?

Life

Look carefully then how you walk, not as unwise but as
wise, making the best use of the time, because the days
are evil. Therefore do not be foolish, but understand what
the will of the Lord is.

EPHESIANS 5:15-17 ESV

When we see the word *therefore* in the Bible, it should teach us
to look back. What was written before our verse that relates to
it? Throughout his letters, Paul implores believers to walk in
a worthy manner and not walk like the rest of the world. The
walk he is speaking of is their very lives, or their Christian
walk, as we say now. Life with God is not a momentary prayer,
but a lifelong journey with God.

As we walk, it is helpful to be reflective. Life is not a sprint;
we don't need to go as fast as we can without looking back or
slowing down. Since life is a journey, there needs to be plenty
of time to pause. When you pause, ask yourself if your life best
reflects Christ or the world. Review your recent actions. Have
they been wise or unwise? Ask if you are using your time for
God's glory, or if your schedule could use some pruning. Let us
be women who reflect backward in order to walk forward better.

Which of these questions will you reflect on today?

Influence

*I am reminded of your sincere faith, a faith that dwelt
first in your grandmother Lois and your mother Eunice
and now, I am sure, dwells in you as well.*

2 TIMOTHY 1:5 ESV

Who are Lois and Eunice? From this verse, we can gather that
they are the grandmother and mother of Timothy, respectively.
If this verse had been omitted from the Bible, however, you
would never know. They don't have a book of the Bible
named after them. They probably didn't go on any missionary
journeys. They are two unknown women, but this sentence
about them speaks volumes. They had faith, and they taught
this faith to their grandson and son, Timothy. They discipled
him in the faith of Christ, and he went on to preach the gospel
and fulfill his calling. They were faithful to disciple those
closest to them and to share their faith. Without Lois and
Eunice, would there be a Timothy? Would Paul have written
two letters to encourage him?

Dear sister, you cannot fathom the great things God wants to do
with what you think is your small circle of influence. Be faithful
in the small, and God will bless it. You are called to share the
gospel and live out your faith, whether you disciple one person
or millions. Maybe you only ever see your kids, grandkids,
nieces, or nephews. It matters. Your influence matters.

*Who is God putting on your heart to remind you that your
spiritual influence matters?*

Honorable

*Keep your conduct among the Gentiles honorable, so that
when they speak against you as evildoers, they may see
your good deeds and glorify God on the day of visitation.*

1 PETER 2:12 ESV

A good parent knows that what their kids see them do often
outweighs what they tell their kids to do. If the parent is
constantly cursing, the child will pick up those words. If a
parent often lies, the child knows their word cannot be trusted.
Actions speak louder than words, the old saying goes.

The early believers who received Peter's letter had been accused
of many things: being terrorists, leading slaves to insurrection,
rebellion against the government, and cannibalism, to name
a few. Peter did not tell the believers to rise and defend their
names. He told them that they were in charge of their response.
Their actions represented something much bigger than
themselves; they were representing Christ. Peter admonished
them to act honorably and bring glory to God. Like the parent
of a child, Peter wanted their actions to speak louder than
any verbal defense they could give. Have you been slandered
or wrongly portrayed? Maybe others consider you weird just
because you believe in Jesus. Don't be discouraged. Continue to
live your life in an honorable manner, giving the glory to God
and knowing that he will reward you.

How would the unbelievers in your life describe your actions?

Lovable

While we were still weak, at the right time Christ died for the ungodly. For one will scarcely die for a righteous person—though perhaps for a good person one would dare even to die—but God shows his love for us in that while we were still sinners, Christ died for us.

ROMANS 5:6-8 NIV

Have you ever felt unloved or unwanted? Maybe you felt like you failed God. Maybe you struggle to love yourself the way you should. Perhaps it was a relationship that undervalued or never appreciated your friendship. Other times, we do things that hurt God and others, building a large case against us being lovable. Thankfully, it's not our strength or good deeds that makes us lovable.

God displayed wild, ardent love for you while you were still in your most unlovable state. When you lived in rejection of him, heart turned away and fully immersed in sin, he looked upon you with fervent love and said, "for her." This crazy love moved the heart of God toward the rescue mission for you. He has pulled you out of the muck and called you his child. He loves you passionately. If you feel unloved because of an earthly relationship, don't stuff your hurt. Bring it to your Father. If you can't find a reason to love yourself, ask God to show you who you are. If you think God has turned his back on you because of your sin, turn your eyes to his Son's nail-pierced hands.

What do you do when you feel unloved?

Intelligent

The fear of the LORD is the beginning of knowledge,
but fools despise wisdom and instruction.
PROVERBS 1:7 NIV

Have you heard the term "intelligent design"? It's used most often in reference to creation. It means that the world was not created by random chance, but that God created it in an intelligent, thought-out manner. God created us in the same way, making us into his very image. This means that he is an intelligent God, and all knowledge and wisdom comes from him.

There is a tendency to disconnect science and God. Some people think that you can't be a Christian and be a good scientist. But the opposite is true! God has given all of us the gift of intellect. We all have different types, be it music, books, science, arts, mechanics, the list goes on and on. These are gifts from God to be used for his glory. We don't need to separate our seemingly secular gifts from our desire to give glory to God. If all good gifts come from him, they can work in harmony together. If you find yourself in a scientific field, don't shy away from both your calling and your desire to serve God. Ask him how he can use your God-given intelligence for his glory.

What knowledge or skill can you praise God for today?

Observant

Be alert and of sober mind. Your enemy the devil prowls around like a roaring lion looking for someone to devour.

1 Peter 5:8 NIV

Do you recognize the attacks on the enemy on your life? There is a very real spiritual realm, and a very real spiritual battle rages there. Once you become a believer, you are sealed, made safe by the Holy Spirit. However, that does not mean the attacks stop. Satan wants nothing more than to make you ineffective for the kingdom of God, and he will attempt to turn your heart from him.

With this knowledge, we believers must be observant to his attacks, aware of his plans. We also must know what our weaknesses are. Are you tempted by a particular sin? That's the plan of the enemy against you. How can you set up vulnerable accountability and prayer regarding that place? Are you struggling in your relationships? Consider that Satan does not want your family to thrive. The plan of attack will look different for each believer.

How can you be alert to a plan of attack?

Peaceful

The LORD gives strength to his people;
the LORD blesses his people with peace.
PSALM 29:11 NIV

If you are thirsty and you want water, you need to draw it from a well that has good water. You can take the water out and put lemon in it, add ice, garnish it with a fancy umbrella, and serve it in a cute cup, but that doesn't mean the water is good. If you want the water to be good, you must check the source. Is the source of the water good?

When it comes to peace, the same is true. We can try to draw our peace from the world, which offers many ways to false peace. The world will tell you to look inside yourself, that you can find peace there. The world will try to tell you if you have more things, or take more time for self-care, then you will have peace. Maybe it will tell you that peace will come once a political party is out of power or a difficult relationship is ended. True and lasting peace does not come from any of these things. Jesus is the only source for true peace. If you want peace, go to the source. Drink of the living water that is Christ, and no matter your circumstances, you will be blessed with peace.

What are you seeking peace in outside of Christ right now?

Obliging

When Moses' hands grew tired, they took a stone and put it under him and he sat on it. Aaron and Hur held his hands up—one on one side, one on the other—so that his hands remained steady till sunset.

EXODUS 17:12 NIV

Obliging is not a word we use much in our vocabulary anymore. It means to be helpful. Consider this story of Moses in Exodus 17. There was an army coming against Israel. Joshua was told to go out into battle, and Moses was to stand on the hill overlooking it, holding his staff above his head. Moses is not a superhuman, so naturally his arms got tired. That did not change the fact that God had commanded him to do something. So, Aaron and Hur held his hands up. What a picture!

Neither of them had been commanded to help, and they probably would not have been held accountable for Moses putting his hands down. His task was not their calling or even their problem, but they supported Moses in what God had called him to do. They helped ensure the victory of Joshua and all his men because they chose to selflessly put the needs of others before themselves. Life is not all about us. Let us find ways to support and be helpful toward others.

Who is God asking you to be a helpful, supportive presence to today?

Recognized

*When he was at the table with them, he took the bread
and blessed it and broke it and gave it to them.
And their eyes were opened, and they recognized him.
And he vanished from their sight. They said to each
other, "Did not our hearts burn within us while he talked
to us on the road, while he opened to us the Scriptures?"*

LUKE 24:30-32 ESV

If you read the entirety of Luke 24, you find that today's verse is from the story of two travelers walking down the road after the resurrection of Jesus. Jesus comes up beside them and essentially plays dumb, asking them what had happened. The account says they did not recognize him. He then explains to them, using all of Scripture, the truth about himself. When the time was right, at the supper table over the bread, he allowed their eyes to be opened.

Many have questioned why Jesus chose to blind their eyes to who he was at first. Though we don't have an answer to that question, there is no doubt that their spirits recognized Jesus. It says that their hearts burned with them at hearing the good news. Have you had this experience? Has your heart burned with passionate love because of the Holy Spirit working in your heart? God is real! Our experience is just one of the many ways we can express to others that he is real. Recognize his presence and praise him for it.

Have you felt this burning? Describe that experience.

Nourishing

"People do not live by bread alone,
but by every word that comes from the mouth of God."
MATTHEW 4:4 NLT

We take the time to feed our bodies. Even if we are running late, we hit up the drive-through and grab breakfast. We diet and meal plan, giving a lot of focus to the food that our body consumes. It's not a bad thing to do so, but let's feed our souls with the same remembrance and fervor with which we feed our physical bodies.

We aren't surprised when we get *hangry* (which is anger as a result of hunger) or weak when we don't eat. Why are we surprised at the direction of our day when we starve our souls? Even this devotional book cannot take priority over grabbing the actual Bible and reading those life-giving words. Let us prioritize Scripture and consume the Word of God each day. One way you can do that is to use the Scripture given daily here and read the whole chapter instead of just the verse given. Another great way is to take the verse here, write it down, and memorize it. Nourish your soul for growth!

Have you been starving your soul? How can you prioritize God's Word?

June

"See, God has come to save me,
I will trust in him and not be afraid.
The LORD GOD is my strength and my song;
He has given me victory."

Isaiah 12:2 NLT

Powerful

How great is our God!
There's absolutely nothing his power cannot accomplish,
and he has an infinite understanding of everything.

PSALM 147:5 ESV

Have you ever driven past fields of solar shields collecting energy? Or those large, white wind turbines? Though impressive to see, without the sun or the wind, they are completely useless. Neither the panel nor the turbine has the power to create energy. The source of the energy comes from the sun or the wind. That is where the true power lies.

Have you ever considered that God wants us to display his power to the earth? When you surrender all to Jesus, your life cannot help but change. Your actions, motives, the way you speak—the Holy Spirit brings real change to a believer's life. In this way, God displays his power to all those around you and all with whom you share your testimony. What kind of power is he showing? The power that conquered sin and death. The power that can redeem. The power that he offers to give us new hearts and transform us into new creations, as only he can. We have the unique opportunity to display the magnificent, awesome power of God to all around us.

How has God's power been displayed in your life?

Qualified

It is not that we think we are qualified to do anything on our own. Our qualification comes from God.

2 CORINTHIANS 3:5 NLT

If you've ever searched for a job, you've probably seen phrases like "college degree required" or "five years experienced preferred." Being new to the workforce can be discouraging. How are you supposed to get experience if no one hires without experience? Many companies don't bother with candidates that are not qualified for the position; it's a liability to them.

God doesn't work that way. In fact, God wants you to acknowledge that you are unqualified! Once we can humbly realize that nothing will be accomplished by our own power, then God sees we are ready to work. That's when his power best shows through us. When we try to accomplish things by pulling ourselves up by our bootstraps and bulldozing through, it's a quick road to burnout and ineffectiveness. We need to be women who see that we can accomplish great things for the Lord and that he equips and qualifies us. Are you stuck? Burned out? Humbly ask God to show you how you might be doing this on your strength instead of his.

What qualification do you gain from God?

Ready

*"Keep watch, because you do not know
the day or the hour."*
MATTHEW 25:13 NIV

When Jesus ascended into heaven, he assured his disciples
of his return. Here, and many other places in Scripture, we
are told that Jesus will return, and we are told to be ready. In
Matthew 25, Jesus communicates this through a few parables.

The first one is the parable of the ten virgins. They were tasked
to wait with their lamps for the bridegroom. Five had oil, and
were ready; five did not, so they missed out. This parable tells
us that we must be prepared for the second coming of the Lord.
Do you consider yourself ready, or do you not give it a second
thought? The return of Jesus should affect our daily lives. It
should help us prioritize how we live and strengthen on our
values. If we value his coming, we will put value into things
like sharing the gospel, prayer, and reading the Bible. Jesus will
return, whether we are ready or not.

How are you wisely using the time you have been given?

Respectable

*Show proper respect to everyone, love the family of
believers, fear God, honor the emperor.*

1 Peter 2:17 esv

In this passage of Scripture, there are four groups mentioned:
everyone, believers, God, and the emperor. The word *respect*
translates to "honor or value." As believers, we are to show
value to everyone. We are to honor our fellow believers, honor
God, and respect government authorities. Above all, we are
called to recognize the value of a human soul. God values each
life created. Every life is more valuable to him than all the riches
this world can offer. We should act likewise.

A mother might tell her children, "People are more important
than things." The person in front of you holds more importance
than any material thing or money. We are to love the church,
regardless of their race, denomination, gender, or personal
opinions. Jesus tells us that the world will know we are his
disciples by how we love each other. Unity and respect in the
church is vital. Lastly, governments are made up of people, too.
Though we are not required to give them the awe and obedience
that is reserved for God alone, God has given governments a
degree of authority.

*Which group of people is hardest for you to respect? What does it
look like for you to respect them?*

Renewed

Do not conform to the pattern of this world, but be transformed by the renewing of your mind. Then you will be able to test and approve what God's will is— his good, pleasing and perfect will.

ROMANS 12:2 NIV

This word *renewing* is used only twice in the entire New Testament. It is used here and in Titus 3:5. In Titus, it speaks about God saving us by the "renewal of the Holy Spirit." Here, we are called to renew our minds. First, we must realize that we need the Holy Spirit to renew our minds. He is essential to this. We should also recognize that we can transform our outer appearances all we want and still not renew our minds.

Paul is not writing about exchanging our bondage to sin for bondage to legalistic rule-following. What he is describing is a radical, Holy Spirit-led, inner transformation of our entire worldview, from one that was bent in rebellion toward God to one that bends its knee to God. What does this look like? It looks like the Holy Spirit leading us to the gospel. To prayer. To Bible study. To meditate on his Word. To beholding the glory of Christ.

Is your life a fake front, outwardly transformed but inwardly decaying? Or are you submitting to the Holy Spirit to renew your mind?

Secure

He lifted me out of the pit of despair,
out of the mud and the mire.
He set my feet on solid ground
and steadied me as I walked along.
PSALM 40:2 NIV

Have you ever played the game where the floor is lava or quicksand? Essentially, the game is to avoid the areas designated as lava or sand. A comedian recently joked that as a kid, they thought quicksand would be a much bigger problem than it really is. While most of us agree with this joke, it's not physical pits, mud, and quicksand that the psalmist is writing about here.

Most can relate to being in spiritual, emotional, or situational muck. Feelings of depression, despair, anxiety, and being stuck are common. In these times, we long to feel the security of solid ground beneath our feet, something to ground us. Jesus is the rock we can stand upon. When the sands of life are shifting and we realize we cannot place our feet upon a career, marriage, family life, political party, or any of the other things we try to find security in, Jesus is there to be our rock. When you feel like you are sinking into depression and doubt, Jesus is there to pull you out. Whatever you face, cry out to him. Let him be your security.

What quicksand do you face?

Sensitive

We who are strong must be considerate of those who are sensitive about things like this. We must not just please ourselves. For even Christ didn't live to please himself.

ROMANS 15.1, 3 NLT

Walk through the gospels, observing the ministry of Jesus, and you find that he was highly sensitive to the needs of others. When the disciples were annoyed by the children around them, Jesus told the children to draw near. The society that Jesus walked in was a patriarchal society. Women often were viewed as lesser, subordinate to men, and spiritually inferior. Jesus broke through this patriarchal mindset and met the needs of the people, regardless of gender. He displayed compassion and did not adhere to the social rules of the time, healing and ministering to women in a way that was unheard of.

Jesus was compassionate toward those on the outskirts of society. He touched lepers, healed the unclean, and noticed the marginalized who society had cast aside. It wasn't just those displaying physical ailments. People hated by others— tax collectors, political zealots, prostitutes—regularly found themselves in the company of Jesus. Jesus came to break down all barriers and walls that humanity has constructed. He is sensitive to others and bold in mercy.

How can we be more like Christ in this area?

Rich

*God is able to bless you abundantly,
so that in all things at all times,
having all that you need,
you will abound in every good work.*

2 CORINTHIANS 9:8 NLT

God has been so generous toward us. He blesses us in so
many ways. Have you ever felt guilty over God's blessings? For
instance, maybe you have had several easy pregnancies while a
friend struggles to get pregnant. You have no financial debt, but
a church member feels like they are drowning in it. You have
a clean bill of health, but your young neighbor just found out
they have cancer.

We could go on and on, making lists of our blessings and
comparing them to the suffering of others. But this is not
what we are supposed to do, and we are not supposed to let
shame steal our joy. God blesses us because he loves us, but
that doesn't mean he loves others less. There are seasons
of abundance and seasons of suffering. In our seasons of
abundance, we can model the generosity of our Lord and help
to alleviate the suffering of others. God is pleased when we help
one another. If you are in a season of abundance, praise God!
May his abundance never frighten you or cause you to compare,
but instead invoke a spirit of generosity within you.

Do you struggle with shame in seasons of goodness?

Transforming

"I will give you a new heart, and a new spirit I will put within you. And I will remove the heart of stone from your flesh and give you a heart of flesh."

 EZEKIEL 36:26 ESV

In the southwest portion of the United States, there is a national park called Joshua Tree. The park is named for its famous trees, but there are also rocks—massive boulders that look as though a giant was playing with marbles and scattered them about. Many people who visit the park like to look at the stones and try to find shapes in them, such as the famous skull rock or the heart rock. We all can agree that the stones are hard and dead, and most are immovable by human strength.

In the same way, we inherited a heart of stone from Adam. These hearts cannot be moved by our own power, but by the power of the Holy Spirit, the great transformation occurs. We exchange our hard, dead-in-sin hearts for new ones. Our new spiritual hearts are made of flesh, full of life, oxygenated by the breath of God and the blood of Jesus Christ. This is the transformation of a believer. Soft hearts are our gift from God.

Thank God for his transforming power and gift of a soft heart today.

Sympathetic

Since then we have a great high priest who has passed through the heavens, Jesus, the Son of God, let us hold fast our confession. We do not have a high priest who is unable to sympathize with our weaknesses, but one who in every respect has been tempted as we are, yet without sin.

HEBREWS 4:14-15 NKJV

What does it mean that Jesus is our high priest? The high priest was the one set apart to mediate between God and man during temple services. The priest was appointed for service from amongst men. The high priest was the one selected from the many to enter the most holy place and offer the sacrifice on the day of atonement. By these sacrifices, the people's sins were temporarily covered until the permanent atonement of the Messiah.

Jesus is the Messiah, the only one who can permanently atone for our sins. He took it a step further by becoming a man, so that he could sympathize with our very weaknesses and temptations. He chose to not be a far-removed savior, grandly swooping in to save us. Instead, he came as a humble baby, so near and close into our human experience, out of love for us. In this way, he knows us intimately. He feels your suffering as his own, and his love cannot be held back from you in your pain. Find comfort in the promise of permanent atonement in the Messiah, the highest priest of all.

What does it mean to you that Jesus sympathizes with you?

Tenacious

*Hannah replied, "I am a woman who is deeply troubled.
I have not been drinking wine or beer; I was pouring
out my soul to the LORD. Do not take your servant for a
wicked woman; I have been praying here out of my great
anguish and grief."*

1 SAMUEL 1:15 NIV

At the beginning of 1 Samuel, we meet Hannah, one of the
most tenacious women in Scripture. Hannah is barren, and
she is at the temple, praying to God to give her a child. She is
in such anguish that the priest thinks she is drunk. She's not
intoxicated; she is determined.

Many of the Bible's stories about persistence and tenacity
are about women. In the New Testament, Jesus tells us the
parable of the persistent widow. Starting at Matthew 15:21,
we hear of a Canaanite woman who begs Jesus to come heal
her daughter. There is also the story in John of the woman
who sought healing from Jesus. She had been ill for twelve
years, and she doesn't let anything come between her and
Jesus. These women are models on how we can persist in
pursuit of what God has laid on our hearts. Your faith will face
some impossible circumstances, just like these women faced
illnesses, barrenness, judgment of others, and social rejection.
Don't give up!

*What are you tempted to give up on? How is God asking you to
continue in tenacious prayer today?*

Treasure

*"Do not lay up for yourselves treasures on earth, where
moth and rust[e]destroy and where thieves break in and
steal, but lay up for yourselves treasures in heaven, where
neither moth nor rust destroys and where thieves do not
break in and steal. For where your treasure is, there your
heart will be also."*

MATTHEW 6:19-21 ESV

Let's first look at this from the angle of what Jesus was not
saying. He wasn't saying that owning possessions is evil. He
wasn't saying we should feel guilty for the gifts that God has
given us, or that we shouldn't enjoy the things we have. Lastly,
he wasn't saying it is wrong to save or invest money.

This statement, like most of the ones he makes in the sermon
of the mount, focuses the listener's ear on the heart. He was
telling them to not covet, to not be selfish, to not pursue the
love of money and material wealth at the expense of their souls.
They shouldn't find their worth in the magnitude of what they
own, but in God. Take treasure hunters, for example. They are a
tenacious bunch who seek one thing—the treasure they desire.
They often come across other valuable things in the pursuit, but
usually their hearts are focused on wealth. In the same way, our
treasure, our hearts' focus, is Christ. He is what we pursue.

*Is your heart in pursuit of one treasure, or are you distracted by
shiny things?*

Upright

The LORD God is a sun and shield;
the LORD bestows favor and honor.
No good thing does he withhold
from those who walk uprightly.

PSALM 84:11 ESV

Here we are, right before the official beginning of summer. Summer days are marked by more sunlight. We enjoy its warmth and vitamin D, and we relish in the extra time we can spend outside. Just like the sun, God is always present to nourish us and enlighten our paths.

This metaphor between God and the sun is nowhere else in the Old Testament. Perhaps the prominence of sun worship at the time rendered it a poor metaphor, but what the psalmist is communicating is that not everyone receives the favor of God. If you live in a basement with no windows, and you never come out, you will never receive the favor of the sun. You live in darkness. But if you go outside, there are many benefits, some of which we already listed. God isn't playing favorites, but those who have faith in his Son that are walking in the light. In Christ, we are those who walk upright, God has many good blessings and honor that he wants to give to you. Bask in the warmth of his love today.

What good thing has God given you lately?

Validated

I praise you, for I am fearfully and wonderfully made.
Wonderful are your works;
my soul knows it very well.

PSALM 139:14 ESV

Do you struggle to see yourself as worthy? Our self-worth should be rooted in God. If you don't find your validation in Christ, you will look elsewhere, and other sources will never bring us true worth. They are all passing and finite; God is eternal. He has created us in his image, giving us value simply by that act. God knows each of us as individual humans. He doesn't look down and see us as faceless waves of humanity. He knows every hair on your head. Who else could name such an obscure number? God values every one of us.

We can look for our value in having children, in expanding a thriving career, in accomplishing a dream, or in making a lot of money. It can even be small, seemingly good things, like having a clean house, daily exercise, or being the one who has her Bible study done on time. Still, any source outside of God that we draw our worth from is empty. Look into the loving, kind eyes of Jesus, and listen to what he has to say about you.

Who does Jesus say that you are?

Uninhibited

*David danced before the LORD with all his might, wearing
a priestly garment. David and all the people of Israel
brought up the Ark of the LORD with shouts of joy and the
blowing of rams' horns.*

2 SAMUEL 6:14-15 NLT

David was a worshiper. The author of the majority of Psalms,
he is well-known for going from a young boy, composing
worship in the company of his sheep, to the king over a
flourishing Israel. On this occasion, David removes his royal
attire and worships before the Lord in his linen garment. Later
in 2 Samuel, it says that his wife watched him with contempt.
While there were a few things at play here, what we do know
is that David was not concerned with what those around him
thought of the display. His heart was focused on worship of the
Lord. He was full of joy at the ark of the covenant's return, and
he could not contain it.

Uninhibited worship. What would it look like if you worshiped
the Lord uninhibited? Shame and fear of other's opinions can
suffocate us if we surrender to them. We are called to live our
lives for an audience of one, meaning that when we worship, it's
for the Lord. If our hearts are full of joy, let us not hold back.
If we mourn in repentance, let us bow a knee. Others will not
always understand. Still, let us worship our God, majestic and
awe-inspiring as he is, with uninhibited praise!

How is fear of others holding you back in worship?

Tremendous

The tongue has the power of life and death,
and those who love it will eat its fruit.
PROVERBS 18:21 ESV

Consider an oceanic ship. The massive vessel, which can carry people or cargo and masterfully cut through the waves, is guided by a tiny part called the rudder. A rudder is a good metaphor for the tremendous power of our words. Our words have power. Not only do they have power, but the Bible tells us that they are an accurate portrayal of our hearts. The Bible says that a righteous person's words are like a fountain of life—discerning, valued like silver, wise, and nourishing to many.

Prayerfully analyze the words you speak. Who do you have the most trouble controlling your tongue around? Is it gossiping with friends when you are feeling insecure? Harsh words toward your kids because you feel out of control? Name-calling with a spouse because they hurt you? Slandering a stranger out of jealousy? There is usually a root for every bitter word we speak, a reason behind the sin. We need to get the heart issue of the words if we want the fruit of our tongues to change. May we be women who use this tremendous power for life and encouragement, not death and destruction.

What words does the Holy Spirit bring to your mind?

Watchful

> *Going a little farther, he fell with his face to the ground and prayed, "My Father, if it is possible, may this cup be taken from me. Yet not as I will, but as you will." Then he returned to his disciples and found them sleeping. "Couldn't you men keep watch with me for one hour?" he asked Peter. "Watch and pray so that you will not fall into temptation. The spirit is willing, but the flesh is weak."*
> MATTHEW 26:38-21 ESV

Jesus is going to the garden to pray. He asks three of his disciples to take watch for him. At first, Jesus is simply asking them to physically stay awake. But when Jesus addresses Peter, he is talking about a different kind of watch. This kind of watchfulness is the spiritual kind.

Being awake in the Bible is often equated with righteousness. This, partnered with prayer, is what helps us to fight against temptation. We need to stay spiritually awake. We need the righteousness of Christ to help us abstain from sin. We need to be in prayer for ourselves and for each other because all flesh is weak. Remember what Paul tells us about this? In our weakness, God's strength shows. Are you struggling in temptation to sin? Get on your knees, sister, and stay awake. God is on the move.

Are you spiritually asleep?

Understood

"Where have you laid him?" he asked.
"Come and see, Lord," they replied.
Jesus wept.
Then the Jews said, "See how he loved him!"
JOHN 11:34-36 NIV

Have you ever felt alone? Loneliness can strike in good times and in bad. Sometimes, we are full of joy and want to share, but there is no one to share it with. Other times, when we are in a discouraging situation, there is nothing better than someone who can relate to what you are going through. You will not always find fulfillment for your loneliness here on earth, but you can be assured that Jesus understands.

Jesus is the friend that sticks close. He will never abandon or reject you, and he has unlimited empathy and compassion for your situations. Jesus knew what it was like to be rejected, as he was rejected by even his closest of friends at one point. He knew what it meant to be misunderstood by family. He knows what it feels like to have his character attacked by strangers. He knew poverty, temptation, weariness, disappointment, and loneliness. If you long for someone to share in your joy and your disappointments, pour out your heart to Jesus. He is near, and he understands.

What comfort do you gather from the fact that Jesus understands?

Optimistic

*We know that in all things God works
for the good of those who love him,
who have been called according to his purpose.*

ROMANS 8:28 NIV

We all need optimistic people in our lives. Maybe you are an optimist. If so, consider yourself valued! Some people think that optimists express false hope, which they can find discouraging. However, if you are a believer, you have reason to be an eternal optimist. The battle over sin and death has already been won, and we know the outcome! If you confess Jesus Christ as your Lord, then you know your eternal outcome as well.

We get to have an unwavering confidence in God, knowing that he is in control of our lives, that he loves and cares for us, that he is working in our lives, and that we will spend eternity with him. We know that he wastes nothing, and that he is infinitely good, so he can work good in every detail of our life. This is unfailing optimism because it's all based on fact. Our hope is a confident hope, a reassured and unfailing hope. So next time you consider if you are a pessimist or an optimist, know that as a believer, you can be an eternal optimist. What good news!

How can you praise God for the hope that he brings you each day?

Passionate

In the temple courts he found people selling cattle, sheep and doves, and others sitting at tables exchanging money. So he made a whip out of cords, and drove all from the temple courts, both sheep and cattle; he scattered the coins of the money changers and overturned their tables. To those who sold doves he said, "Get these out of here! Stop turning my Father's house into a market!" His disciples remembered that it is written: "Zeal for your house will consume me."

JOHN 2:14-17 NIV

The terms *zeal* and *passion* are often used interchangeably in the Bible. In today's reading, Jesus enters the temple right before Passover and finds a sight that stirs him to action. You see, Jesus was passionate about people being able to connect with the Father. The money changers and merchants were getting in the way of people doing that very thing. That is why Jesus took the drastic action that he did. Nothing was more important to him.

What are you passionate about? What needs in the church or in your community bring compassion up in you or make you upset? What change do you wish to see in the world? Be that change. God created each of us with unique gifts and passions. It's okay to be zealous in pursuit of those. Many will try to deter you or tell you to calm down. Keep following the Holy Spirit. Don't mind what they say!

What are you passionate about?

Pleasing

When people's lives please the LORD,
even their enemies are at peace with them.

PROVERBS 16:7 NLT

If children are trying to please their parents, they might make sure they eat all their vegetables and clean their room when told. At work, an employee will work harder when they want to please the boss or client. No matter the relationship, trying to please someone usually requires extra effort, going above and beyond.

With God, people have varying ideas on what pleases him. Living a morally upright life must please him. Or perhaps it's reading the whole Bible every year. Praying five times a day, fasting, confession, good deeds, sacrifice—these are all ways that man attempts to please God. Though those things are not bad in and of themselves, they don't work. Nothing we can do works. What God requires us of us is faith in his Son. That's what pleases him. Faith. Those other things can bring us closer to God once we are saved, and they can help our spiritual development, but they can never be the way God is pleased with us. He looks upon you, sees you in Christ, and is pleased. He is pleased with you! Be blessed in this.

Do you try harder to make God pleased with you, or do you know he is pleased?

Prudent

A fool despises his father's instruction,
but whoever heeds reproof is prudent.
PROVERBS 15:5 ESV

Not all of us grew up with loving earthly fathers. Some of them got discipline wrong or didn't try to discipline at all. Maybe your father wasn't even around to give instruction. Did you know that the Bible says God the Father disciplines those he loves? God is perfect, which means that he gets discipline perfect as well. He corrects us and gives us instruction out of love.

God wants good for us. Sometimes, for good to come, we must be disciplined like children. It can be hard to receive, especially if we did not have earthly fathers who instructed us well. You may be hardened to reproof and correction. The writer of Proverbs says to ignore such discipline makes us fools. It's true; the longer we ignore the correction of the Lord, the harder our hearts become. To be prudent is to be thoughtful about your future. By listening to the Father, even when it is hard, you show submission and can remove yourself from many troubles.

Do you know what the discipline of the Lord looks like in your life?

Refreshment

Repent and return, so that your sins may be wiped away,
in order that times of refreshing may come
from the presence of the Lord.
ACTS 3:19 NASB

After a long, hard winter, there is nothing like the first day that it creeps back above freezing. The wind feels warm, the snow begins to melt, and the souls of everyone are uplifted at the thought of the warmth to come. The air meets your lungs with sweet joy instead of the harshness of the cold.

This refreshing transition into spring is like the refreshing that comes from the presence of God after repentance. Our sins have been equated to filthy rags in the Bible. The scent of our sinful lives would not be considered pleasant in the least. When we repent of these sins, it's a breath of fresh air. Jesus cleanses us of our sins, and the breath of the Holy Spirit sweeps through our souls. It's a beautiful picture. And then, the relief. The relief comes from the smell of freedom in the air. Just like spring after a hard winter, the freedom that Christ brings when we repent is beautiful. Praise God for the winds of spring!

Spend some time prayerfully repenting and accept the refreshment of the Lord.

Relevant

*When Jesus saw the crowds, he went up on a
mountainside and sat down. His disciples came to him,
and he began to teach them.*

MATTHEW 5:1 NIV

When you study Jesus' life, you notice that he interacts
differently with different people. He doesn't come to the
lame man and speak to him in the same way that he interacts
with the woman at the well. Jesus meets each person in their
individual need, even though the core of his message is the
same. Though we were sinners, Christ died for us, and he has
set us free from the bondage of sin and death.

There are approximately seven billion people on this earth,
from all different nations, speaking over seven thousand
languages, and ranging in age from newborn to over a hundred
years old. Even with these many factors and variables, the core
of the gospel is the same for every one of them. How we present
the gospel, however, can adapt. Just like Jesus compassionately
met a person in their need and situation, we need to do the
same. For some, he spoke more directly. For others, he spoke
in parables. He brought up the sinful pasts of some. In other
cases, he just healed their physical ailments and spoke of their
hearts later.

*How can you bring the core gospel in a relevant way to someone
who needs to hear it today?*

Friendship

*Sweet friendships refresh the soul
and awaken our hearts with joy,
for good friends are like the anointing oil
that yields the fragrant incense of God's presence.*

PROVERBS 27:9 TPT

Have you heard of this trick to use when trying to sell your house? Before showings, put some cookies in the oven. Then, when people come for the showing, the whole house smells like freshly baked cookies, invoking feelings of home. Smell, one of our five senses, is important to memory and brain function. One sniff and we can be transported, from mowed grass and falling rain to pool chlorine and moth balls. Smells bring up memories and emotions.

Imagine how Mary, Martha's sister, felt when she anointed the feet of Jesus with expensive perfume. Perhaps later in her life, she passed by the market and smelled that same fragrance, a reminder of her friendship with her Savior. This begs the question, what fragrance do you leave with people? Are you a refreshing friend? We can be refreshing by listening well, thinking about our friends' needs, and always pointing them back to Jesus. In the same way, God gives us friends to encourage us in our walk with him.

Are you the type of friend who leaves the fragrance of God?

Glorious

*"The glory that you have given me I have given to them,
that they may be one even as we are one, I in them and
you in me, that they may become perfectly one, so that
the world may know that you sent me and loved them
even as you loved me."*

JOHN 17:22-23 ESV

In your Bible reading, you've probably come across the word *glory* many times. But what does the glory of God really mean? The glory of God is multifaceted, but it is the beauty of his spirit. This is not necessarily a physical beauty, but rather the beauty of all that he is; his character is beautiful. The glory of God is eternal. In John 17, Jesus states that he is giving us the glory that the Father has given him. What an immense gift! But what does that mean?

The glory he gives us is his Spirit. Those of us living in the church age, the time after the resurrection of Christ, have the distinct privilege of the Holy Spirit living inside of us. We are vessels that carry the glory of God. God knew that we would need him to take his love to the ends of the earth. We display how glorious God is. Just like the sight of a magnificent mountain range or crashing ocean waves can lead a person to God, so too can our lives.

How do you feel knowing that you are a vessel containing the glory of God?

Fervent

*Peter, therefore, indeed, was kept in the prison,
and fervent prayer was being made
by the assembly unto God for him.*

ACTS 12:5 ESV

When we think of being fervent, the thought of all-night prayer meetings and passionate, loud cries might come to mind. This might lead us to believe that what matters most is how or what we pray. Perhaps if our prayers aren't in a certain fashion, they won't appease God, and he won't hear them and grant our requests. However, the placement of the word *fervent* is important. Fervent prayer is also mentioned in James 5:16. In James, the word means the outcome of the prayer, not necessarily the prayer itself. It is saying that prayer is powerful and should be done.

Here in Acts, Peter was in prison. Even though he was in prison, he was not forgotten. The church was praying for him to be released. Here, the word used for *fervent* is translated to "continuously." In other parts of Scripture, we are told to pray continuously. This is not a measure of time, but a submission of all things to God. The church was submitting to God their request for Peter to be released, and it was answered! The point is, pray. Pray about all things. Submit them to God and see the awesome works he does.

How is your prayer life?

Independent

Each time he said, "My grace is all you need. My power
works best in weakness." So now I am glad to boast
about my weaknesses, so that the power of Christ can
work through me.

2 CORINTHIANS 12:9 ESV

Modern culture encourages us to be independent women
and praises such people. You would be hard-pressed to find
any Bible verses that state as such. In fact, dependence is the
theme you will find most often. Does God help those who help
themselves? That's not from Scripture. Scripture states that God
helps those who cannot help themselves, those who realize that
they need him, and that goes for both women and men.

God created us to be dependent on him and in relationship
with others. The Trinity itself exists in relationship, God as
three in one. This is the design that God has for us. If you
pride yourself in being an independent person or prize the
ability to pull yourself up by your own bootstraps, it might be
time to reevaluate. True humility, which we are called to walk
in, admits that it needs God and others. Not only do you need
others, but others need you! God wants to provide for you,
protect you, and be in relationship with you. He also wants you
to share your needs with others.

How does what the Bible says about being an independent woman
change your views?

Judicious

*"Do not judge by appearances,
but judge with right judgment."*

JOHN 7:24 ESV

Let's say it louder for those in the back; God doesn't judge the outside! He is focused on the heart. With this being said time and time again in Scripture, why do we tend to focus on the outward? We are driven to clean up all our outward actions. We put extreme focus on our outward morality, neglecting the roots. We look at others and, based on their dress and grooming, sum them up and categorize them.

It seems like we humans are bent on being the opposite of judicious. However, by the power of the Holy Spirit, we can renew our minds to judge others rightly. If God judges by the heart, we should, too. This takes more of an effort on our part, as we cannot see a person's heart as God can. We can, however, take what we know from Scripture about the reflections of the heart and apply that. Let us not approach judgment with boldness and pride, as though we excel in this function. Let us approach it with humility. As the saying says, "there, but for the grace of God, go I."

What do you normally base your judgment on?

Lasting

The Lord is not slow in keeping his promise,
as some understand slowness.
Instead he is patient with you,
not wanting anyone to perish,
but everyone to come to repentance.

2 PETER 3:9 NIV

There are many videos and articles about how to have a lasting marriage. Some interview couples who have been married a long time to get their advice. Others turn to science and try to turn it into a formula. Unfortunately, there is no set formula to make any relationship last.

God knows what it means to make a lasting covenant. He is faithful to his promises and takes them very seriously. He does not back out or falter on them. We may look at our world and wonder why Jesus has not come back yet; he promised that he would. But God has a plan, and that plan includes every one of us. He wants to give the opportunity of repentance to everyone. What a blessing! In other promises, we may wish that God would hurry up or keep his word the way we think he should. We can be grateful that God is the expert at keeping lasting promises, and we can rely on him.

What comfort does God's covenant with mankind bring you?

July

*He gives power to the weak
and strength to the powerless.*

ISAIAH 40:29 NLT

Justified

Since we have been justified by faith,
we have peace with God through our Lord Jesus Christ.

ROMANS 5:1 NIV

It's the middle of summer, and school is out, but we are going to have a little language lesson. What are the terms for the three tenses of salvation? If you answered justification, sanctification, and glorification, you are right! To be justified indicates the past tense of salvation. Justification is what happened on the cross. It is Jesus paying the penalty for our sin and reconciling us to God. Sanctification is the present tense. This is the continuation of justification, or the day-to-day process of the Holy Spirit making us more like Christ.

Glorification is the future tense. It is the promise of what we have in the future, when we will be glorified like Christ. All these big terms mean that you have been set free! You have been given peace with God. There is nothing between you and God now. Enjoy the beauty of his presence and the wonders of this peace today.

What does it mean to you to be justified?

Faithful

Let's hold firmly to the confession of our hope without wavering, for He who promised is faithful.

HEBREWS 10:23 NASB

A teenaged driver is taking her driving exam. She needs to pass, and this is one of the very few times she has been on the highway. Nervous, she grips the steering wheel tightly, so tightly that her knuckles turn white. Eventually, she calmed down as she became accustomed to the road, but at the beginning, she held on like her life depended on it.

We need to have this same tight grip on our hope. We can hold onto the promises of God like our very lives depend on it, because they do. We can hold tight, knowing he has us tighter. He will never go back on his word, never forsake his promises. If that young driver had begun to falter, the instructor would have taken over. In the same way, Jesus is faithful, even when you are not. He holds tight, even if your grip fails. It's not our faithfulness that we depend on; it's his.

How have you felt God hold fast to you in times when you wanted to let go?

Eternal

What no eye has seen, nor ear heard,
nor the heart of man imagined,
what God has prepared for those who love him.
1 CORINTHIANS 2:9 ESV

We all daydream. When we do, our thoughts can be filled with the utmost beauty, the greatest possibilities, and images beyond our wildest imagination. We place ourselves in scenarios that fulfill everything we have ever wished for and satisfy our every desire. But alas, it is just a dream. All too soon, we come back to our imperfect reality.

We may acknowledge that life is good, that we are thankful for the blessings God has given us, and yet yearn for more. What is it that leaves our hearts feeling like things aren't quite as they should be? As believers in Christ, we were made for more. We were made to know him, to have an intimate relationship with him. Ultimately, we were made for another world, a world of exquisite beauty that has no comparison. In that world, we will spend every day in the presence of our almighty, loving Lord and Savior.

Who do you feel called to share the good news of salvation in Christ and eternal life with?

Freedom

If we confess our sins, He is faithful and just to forgive us
our sins and to cleanse us from all unrighteousness.

1 JOHN 1:9 NKJV

Some of the decisions and choices we make have consequences that lead us to feel like our very souls are imprisoned. We repeatedly relive the thought process that led us to where we are. If only, what if? We plead for a second chance, but the die is cast. There is no turning back from the results have already arrived.

What if we could find release? We could get over the regret, forget the past, and move on to better things. Can we erase the scene that keeps replaying and live unencumbered? Hallelujah, yes! There is an answer, and it dates back over two thousand years to a hill on Calvary. There, the Son of God gave his life. As he was battered, beaten, and bruised beyond recognition, the resolution was set in stone. Death was defeated, and our transgressions were paid for, giving us the chance to be forgiven and never again remember those sins once confessed. This is the greatest freedom of all.

How often do you truly ponder the lengths Jesus went to in order to save you? Start a habit of daily gratitude for your salvation.

Grit

Be alert and of sober mind. Your enemy the devil prowls
around like a roaring lion looking for someone to devour.
Resist him, standing firm in the faith. And the God of
all grace...will himself restore you and make you strong,
firm and steadfast.

1 PETER 5:8-10 NIV

Full of tenacity and teeth clenched, you are determined to overpower the difficulty you are facing. It takes strength to face some of the hands that life deals. You tell yourself that you can do it. You surround yourself with friends to spur you on to success. And just when you think you have made it, the road gets tougher. The mental games begin. You find yourself not only gearing up physically and mentally; your emotions have gone out of control. As you consider your situation, it dawns on you. You let the enemy of your soul in, and he wants to destroy you.

Do a deep dive into the Word and your grit on! Be on guard for our enemy, who will try to take us down at every opportunity. God gives us the solution, to stand strong and steadfast in faith. We are overcomers in Christ. In him, we have the power to be victorious.

What guards can you incorporate into your daily life?

Exuberant

Delight yourself in the LORD,
and he will give you the desires of your heart.

PSALM 37:4 ESV

Do you remember waiting for Christmas morning as a child? Relive the magical feelings that bubbled up when you saw a present, with your name on it, under the tree. You were full of hope over what that box contained. What about the delight you feel when picking out a gift for someone special in your life? You think long and hard about what they would want, and you imagine how they will open it and be thrilled at your considerate selection. As you anticipate the joy you would be giving to a dear one, you overflow with exuberance yourself.

These are the heartfelt feelings of a heavenly father who wants us to have the desire of our hearts, and he tells us exactly how to get them. We are to delight ourselves in him through worship, praise, gratitude, and obedience. We are to engage in consistent relationship with him and love him with all our hearts. As we do, he will lavish us with the desires we take to him in prayer.

In what ways do you find yourself consistently delighting
in the Lord?

Moving

> *The earth was without form and void, and darkness was over the face of the deep. And the Spirit of God was hovering over the face of the waters.*
>
> GENESIS 1:2 ESV

Pitch darkness. The earth waited for the hand of God to do the miraculous. Can you imagine being present at the creation of the world? Imagine the flashes, the shifting earth, the presence of God moving and manifesting a world that would soon be inhabited by all kinds of living creatures, landscape and vegetation, and the people who would bear his image.

Can you see the light separated from the dark? Close your eyes and visualize the animals great and small. Breathe and remember the first air that filled Adam's lungs, breathed directly from the one true God who designed him. As God made his way through the days of creation, he had you in mind. As the perfect Father, he established a place where you could live a life surrendered to him before spending your eternity at his side. You convinced him to send his only Son to die in your place so that you could be saved. When he moved, it was for you.

Can you thank God today for moving on your behalf, creating, saving, and loving you so magnificently?

Perseverance

Do you not know that in a race all the runners run, but only one gets the prize? Run in such a way as to get the prize. Everyone who competes in the games goes into strict training. They do it to get a crown that will not last, but we do it to get a crown that will last forever.

1 CORINTHIANS 9:24-25 NIV

If you ever played a sport, you can recall a coach telling you to hustle. Can you remember hearing your mom tell you to move it or you would be late for school? Maybe it's a boss who is advising you that you need to work a little smarter and harder. Whatever we do in life, it will not be at its best if we don't put all our effort into it. It might end up okay, but it won't be anything to write home about. There will be a loss of satisfaction and possibly the achievement or degree you needed to move to the next level.

Scripture tells us how to live life on this earth, and it is with persistent determination. We were made to work, disciplining ourselves to keep our eyes on the prize as we accomplish the goal. What is our goal? Our heavenly pursuit is to obtain the eternal crown that will never perish and hear our Lord say, "Well done."

What areas of your life need more spiritual discipline to fulfill the purpose God has for you?

Prayerful

I pray that you and all God's holy people will have the power to understand the greatness of Christ's love—how wide and how long and how high and how deep that love is.

EPHESIANS 3:18 NCV

Can you remember a time when you struggled to comprehend a concept in class? You mustered all your intellect, wanting to know the subject and perceive the inner workings and thought process behind its substance. Although you gave it all you had, you still couldn't grasp the information. What was the key you needed to unlock the insight?

We have all heard the saying that there is power in prayer, but we have barely scratched the surface of that truth. We have the Holy Spirit's power to have great understanding of his Word and the grandness of his love for us. We may not understand everything on this earth, but one day we will see clearly. Someday, when we look into the eyes of Jesus, we will see the enormity of his love. Until then, we must pray for ourselves and one another, that we might know God's love to the extent that we urgently want to share it with others.

If you were called upon to explain God's love for mankind, how would you describe it?

Persuasive

*In your hearts revere Christ as Lord. Always be prepared
to give an answer to everyone who asks you to give
the reason for the hope that you have. But do this with
gentleness and respect.*

1 PETER 3:15 NIV

Have you ever imagined holding an elite position, whether that
be a political seat or the head of a large corporation? It probably
felt exciting yet daunting. You would have to be an expert in
leading, advising, and making critical decisions. What kind of
leader you would be? Harsh or kind, approachable or aloof,
respected or feared?

In God's Word, we are told to have respect for leaders in our
lives. Maybe it is a smaller picture of what we need to do on a
bigger scale to revere Jesus. We should represent Jesus in such a
way that people notice. We are to be ready at all times to answer
questions about who our Savior is and what his salvation
means for life here and in eternity. We are told to share this
truth with gentleness and respect. It is by far the greatest hope
and answer for mankind. It is our calling to be thoroughly
prepared in heart, mind, and spirit to deliver the good news.

*Do you have a plan for studying and sharing the Word of God so
that you can give an answer for your hope?*

Noble

*You were taught to be made new in your hearts,
to become a new person. That new person is made
to be like God—made to be truly good and holy.*

EPHESIANS 4:23-24 NCV

Have you ever felt like you just don't measure up? Maybe you were always picked last for a school sport or sweated it out as you waited to be asked to the prom. Maybe you thought a certain event you wanted to happen in your life never would, and you were the one holding it back. Possibly, you hoped you could rewind life and have things turn out differently.

We all need to stop and praise God. In Christ, we have the opportunity to become new beings. We are called to a new life, one that nothing on this earth can compare to, and it is offered freely to us in exchange for our hearts. When understood, the invitation to this new life sends people to kneel at the feet of Jesus. How will others know that they have this opportunity for transformation? By watching our lives lived out for Christ. Through the power of the Holy Spirit, we can live holy lives that speak volumes to the unsaved of our great salvation.

When people see you, do you think they see the difference Jesus has made in your life?

Proper

Let go of the lifestyle of the ancient man, the old self-life, which was corrupted by sinful and deceitful desires that spring from delusions.

EPHESIANS 4.22 TPT

Have you ever thought about how much better life would be if many people had an attitude adjustment? It's those pesky individuals who often speak and act in a way that grates on you. As your grandma would have said, "They don't have the good horse sense God gave them!" Therein lies the problem. Human beings can see things so differently. We like things done and presented in particular ways. Left to our own interpretation, we could always conclude that we are right, and others are dead wrong.

This is why God's way is the only true way. We can't speak or engage with others with the right actions or intentions unless we are led by the Holy Spirit. If we surrender to God and allow his Spirit to refine and fill us, we will see those who annoy us differently, and we will be the unifying aroma of Christ.

When you interact with others, do you tend to be judgmental or accepting of the differences that may exist between you?

Stamina

The LORD himself goes before you and will be with you;
he will never leave you nor forsake you. Do not be afraid;
do not be discouraged.

DEUTERONOMY 31:8 NIV

There are situations in life where we have to fly solo. No one else can do it for us. Maybe it's giving a speech, taking a driver's test, or undergoing a dreaded medical procedure. The only thing that would stop the event is your absence. You have never felt more necessary or unaided. You try to avoid thinking about the coming dependence on your presence. It's like humming loudly so you won't hear something you don't want to. When the fear creeps in, you do your best deny its whispers.

As believers in Christ, we never, ever go anywhere alone. God's presence is always with us; his eyes are always on his beloved child. There is no reason for fear, anxiety, or discouragement. Wherever we are going, he has already been there to prepare the way. Knowing he is always working for our good can eliminate any concern for those who belong to Jesus.

How can you grow in confidence knowing that God is always with you, continually working on your behalf?

Supportive

Always be humble and gentle.
Be patient with each other,
making allowance for each other's faults
because of your love.

EPHESIANS 4:2 NLT

Pet owners know how unconditional our furry friends' love for us can be. However, there are times in our lives when we just want someone with bare skin to accept us, warts and all. We know we aren't always perfect, and we want others to understand that without passing judgement or withholding affection. If they receive us with a kind and humble approach, it brings healing to our souls.

Scripture makes it very clear that members of the body of Christ must be clothed in humility and kindness, approaching all situations with patience. We must remember how much Jesus has forgiven us, and we are to forgive others in the same fashion. Let's support one another by putting the needs and concerns of others ahead of our own, loving our brothers and sisters in Christ as he has loved us.

When a friend or acquaintance entrusts you with their problem, how can you best use your God-given abilities to help in a gracious way?

Royalty

*You are a chosen people, a royal priesthood, a holy
nation, God's special possession, that you may declare
the praises of him who called you out of darkness into his
wonderful light.*

1 Peter 2:9 niv

The prince rode up on his mighty steed, rescued the maiden
from the evil ogre, and took her to his magnificent castle. He
asked her to be his bride and made her the future queen of
his kingdom. Did you have that dream growing up? Did you
picture your prince, so handsome and strong, the answer to
everything? Could you see your marriage day, the entire village
looking on while a ring was placed on your finger and a crown
on your head? You would always belong to the prince and live
happily ever after.

Just as the prince chose his princess, God has chosen you.
In Christ, he has claimed you as his treasured possession,
delivered you from the powers of darkness, brought you into
his glorious light. You are a child of the King, royal and holy.
Sing praises to his great and almighty name for all he has done
to make you his own.

*Today, how will you show your gratitude to God for making you
his child?*

Vibrant

Sing to him, sing praise to him;
tell of all his wonderful acts.

1 CHRONICLES 16:9 NIV

Picture the brilliant dawning of a new morning, the sun slowly rising with its radiant glory and bringing another day of life to the world. That is something to celebrate. A sunset, wild with color that paints the sky with vivid expression, is powerful to behold. Sitting under the stars, pointing out the shining spectacle of the Milky Way and each shooting star, is a moment of wonder.

To know that there is a creator who made this possible, who conceived this visual masterpiece before bringing it into being, is more than awe-inspiring. Oh Lord, your works are marvelous! Your creation sings your praises. Your people lift their hands in praise and bow down in humble worship, for you are worthy. We wait for the day when we will stand before your throne and worship you day and night for eternity. Come, Lord Jesus, come.

As you praise and worship your Lord, how can you be consciously aware of his presence throughout your day?

Warm

> There the angel of the LORD appeared to him in flames of
> fire from within a bush. Moses saw that though the bush
> was on fire it did not burn up.
>
> EXODUS 3:2 NIV

Have you ever witnessed a natural phenomenon? It could be
beautiful, like the northern lights, or a bit dangerous, like
volcanic lightning. Did it engage you and if so, did you dare to
get close to the spectacle, or did you keep your distance?

Moses encountered a miraculous event in the burning bush.
Have you ever put yourself in his sandals and wondered how
you would have reacted? Would the warmth of the fire invite
you? Or would you run away from this strange bush that didn't
burn? Whether curious or careless, Moses approached the
blaze and met the angel of the Lord. This is when God revealed
his calling on Moses's life. He would lead his chosen people
out of Egypt and into the Promised Land. God appeared in a
miraculous way to Moses. Since Scripture says the Lord is the
same yesterday, today and forever, keep your eyes open for your
burning bush. All things are possible with God.

*How do you really view God? Do you believe his character fully
and have faith in his miraculous ways?*

Whole

> *"What good will it be for someone to gain the whole world, yet forfeit their soul? Or what can anyone give in exchange for their soul?"*
>
> MATTHEW 16:26 NIV

Money, material possessions, power, fame. These aren't only pursued by the rich and famous; some people spend their entire lives chasing after them without success. They have a voracious hunger that is never filled. They want to make their mark and be known for their accomplishments. If they find some level of success, it's not enough. There is always an urge to strive for more. When a millionaire is asked if their money made them happy, most of the time they say no. Many admit that climbing the ladder of success wasn't done with moral fiber, and guilt resulted from too many bad compromises.

There is nothing more important to gain in this life than a relationship with the Son of God. We live in a temporal world where the only everlasting piece is the people made in God's image. Everything else will pass away.

Consider what you spend your time and money on. Is it eternal or temporal?

Valor

> "Be strong and courageous, and act; do not fear nor
> be dismayed, for the LORD God, my God, is with you.
> He will not fail you nor forsake you until all the work
> for the service of the house of the LORD is finished."
>
> 1 CHRONICLES 28:20 NASB

Have you ever been really excited about an opportunity? In your head, you dig your heels in and go for it with gusto. Back in reality, you question yourself, leading to disillusionment about the great prospect ahead of you. You start to wonder if you even want to attempt it or if someone else might be better suited for the task. So, you shrink back. Afterward, you wonder why you couldn't summon the courage. How will you rise from this incident and improve for the next?

As servants of Christ, we never have to wonder where our courage will come from. We know our empowerment is from God. He is fully able to accomplish anything. As we put our faith in him, there is no need to fear; he faithfully moves us in the direction of triumphal victory. Always going before us, behind us and beside us, our Lord will finish every aspect of the purpose he has called us to.

The next time you come up against difficulties, where will you find your strength?

Wisdom

If any of you lacks wisdom, you should ask God,
who gives generously to all without finding fault,
and it will be given to you.

JAMES 1.5 NIV

We encounter so many crossroads in life. We have decisions
demanding answers from us daily. Easy ones are in the black
and white category, but enter the gray area and you may be
tempted to compromise your beliefs. Some choices are common
sense; some require fervent prayer. What if you had the ability
to discern and judge each situation properly as to what is true
and right? To do that, you need wisdom.

Scripture highly values wisdom. The Word says that nothing
we desire can compare with wisdom and that by gaining it, we
will be the ones who benefit. It is more precious than rubies.
By it, we can multiply our days and add years to our lives. A
sign of wisdom is knowing that God's Word is absolute truth.
God wants us to have wisdom, and he offers to give it to us in
abundance if we will only believe. When we ask, we ask in faith,
not doubting, waiting in certainty to receive it.

If God offered you anything, any physical or spiritual gift, what
would you desire most?

Zealous

*Never be lacking in zeal,
but keep your spiritual fervor,
serving the Lord.*

ROMANS 12:11 NIV

When we are devoted to something, we feel inspired, and it moves us to action. We all know the difference between engaging with something important to us and finishing a daily task. We don't tire of working toward what matters deeply to us. Instead, we passionately roll up our sleeves with diligent enthusiasm.

Cultivating our relationship with Christ takes more than reading the Word occasionally and praying when we face a problem. It takes daily commitment. When we move in service to God with earnestness, we will see fruit that glorifies him. When we are diligent in desiring to become more like his Son, it blesses God and brings him pleasure. When Jesus gave his life on the cross for us, there was no question about his devotion to see it through. He suffered severely, but the result was salvation that brought forgiveness and eternal life to us. Christ is our example, and through him, we can live a life that never lacks zeal for the gospel.

What do you need to give up in your life to find time to pursue your relationship with Christ?

Unity

He has given us this command:
Anyone who loves God
must also love their brother and sister.

1 JOHN 4:21 NIV

In the garden, God said, "It is not good for man to be alone," and the recognition of our need for relationship began. As God knit us together in the womb, he placed the deep need to have friendship, family, and a partner to do life with, laugh with, and cry with. When life lacks companionship, we can feel discouraged, lonely, and even experience medical issues. God intended for us to be his body, a community and family of believers who engage with one another on a regular basis, lift one another up, pray for each other, and bear one another's burdens.

Most of all, he wants us to love one another continually. Our heavenly Father is the definition of love. When we love one another, we identify ourselves as children of God. When we don't love, it is a red flag that we may not be following God. We need to examine ourselves, praying that God will give us a sincere heart of love for his church and for all we encounter.

Is there anyone in your life you have trouble loving? If so, will you ask God to help you today?

Valued

> *"On the day when I act," says the LORD Almighty, "they will be my treasured possession. I will spare them, just as a father has compassion and spares his son who serves him."*
>
> MALACHI 3:17 NIV

There are times in life when we wonder what someone else thinks of us. Sometimes, it is an unknown. Other times, a person may make it very clear how they view us. We want to be liked; we want to be accepted. When our identity or our worth is in question, it rocks our world.

We know that Jesus gave his life for us, and there is no greater love than that. However, we humans often need a reminder of how much we mean to him. Let's remind ourselves. God loves us with an everlasting love. He chose us. He sent his only Son to die in our place and offered us forgiveness and salvation. He calls us his treasured possession. He provides for us, goes before us, and fights our battles. He is always working for our good and has a future hope for us. We are his royal priests, and as his bride, we will live in heaven with him forever in his glorious kingdom. What value he has placed on us through the life of his one and only Son!

Do you struggle with believing that God truly loves and values you? Reflect on where his love is shown in your life, in big and small ways.

Strong

*Watch, stand fast in the faith,
be brave, be strong.*
1 CORINTHIANS 16:13 NKJV

We have a culture that is hooked on working out and looking great. Constant advertisements show us the latest exercise programs and newest breakthroughs in supplements and protein powders. If you don't follow their programs, you are ignoring what is intended for your best you. You are acting as your body's enemy, taking it down with every missed sit-up. We know being healthy is God's desire for us, and taking care of our temples is vital, but moderation is key.

God's Word talks about a different kind of strength, one that seeks to protect your physical body, mind, and soul as well. We are to be on guard against the enemy, Satan, who is out to kill, steal, and destroy. We are to keep watch as a soldier guarding their post. We wear God's uniform with our shield of faith and the armor of God. And we are to be brave, for we know that we do not fight this battle on our own. Our faithful God will fight it for us.

Read Ephesians 6 to review the armor of God. How can these tools help you prepare for spiritual battle?

Creative

God created human beings in his own likeness.
He created them to be like himself.
He created them as male and female.

GENESIS 1:2 NLT

The highest and greatest creative mind in existence designed you. Consider the intricacy of each cell and nerve, bones, muscles, skin, and organs that work together as an orchestra to make the body sing a melody of life. How did he design something so exquisite and medically technical at the same time? What was going through his mind as he gave us different shapes and hues, different abilities, and personalities? Whatever it was, the result is magnificent, for God patterned us after himself.

We have never seen God, yet we imagine him. We bear his image, as does every other human being we meet. Take that in for a minute. Do you treat every person you meet as one made in the image of God? If not, this is a wake-up call to understand that God wants us to respect and love all who bear his likeness. Next time you see someone who you might have an opinion about, favorable or not, remind yourself that they are God's image. See how differently you feel.

Do you treat everyone as if they were made in God's image? If not, how can you change that?

Courteous

Though I am free from all,
I have made myself a servant to all,
that I might win more of them.

1 CORINTHIANS 9:19 ESV

Chameleons change their skin to adapt to their surroundings.
People pleasers do anything for others to like them. Compulsive
liars can spin their yarns to embellish on their lives or just
entertain whoever is nearby. For the lizard, adapting is his
nature. In the other two examples, some say these actions are a
choice and some would call them psychological conditions.

As a servant of Christ, your servitude stems from a position of
freedom but your actions are a result of your heart. Your love
for Jesus and gratitude for how he took your place on the cross
moves you to give yourself for the good of others. You are not
forced to do it; your love for your Savior is all the motivation
you need to catapult you into caring for those around you. The
goal is to lay our lives on his altar so we may win lost souls for
Christ. Now, that's a goal worth aiming for daily! Pray to God
for the strength and compassion needed to achieve it.

Are there areas of your life that you have not given over to God
for his use and good purpose?

Affection

*The Lord set his affection on your ancestors and loved
them, and he chose you, their descendants, above all the
nations—as it is today.*

DEUTERONOMY 10:15 NIV

Genealogies are very popular today. There are companies who
sell DNA kits that can tell you who your ancestors were and
various other aspects of your biological history, all from a swab
of the inside of your cheek. The fascination of finding out who
we are and where we came from has made these companies
quite successful.

These genetic tests cannot tell you if your ancestors were
believers in Christ or not, but the Old Testament has many
true stories about your spiritual ancestors. There are accounts
in the Word that reveal God's promise to patriarchs Abraham,
Isaac, and Jacob about how their descendants would be
unnumberable. His Word contains your spiritual heritage.
You can be certain that, even if you don't know your ancestors'
beliefs, you are the chosen of God, and you are sealed in him
through Christ.

*Since there is so much to learn from the lives of our spiritual
ancestors, could you consider committing more time to learn
from their accounts in God's Word?*

Careful

It is the LORD your God you must follow,
and him you must revere.
Keep his commands and obey him;
serve him and hold fast to him.

DEUTERONOMY 13:4 NIV

One sweltering summer night, a young teenage boy was out on a date with a beautiful young girl, enjoying a walk through their neighborhood. The boy thought it would be refreshing to take a swim. His parents did not have a pool, but his neighbors did. The sign on the gate said, "No Trespassing." The boy insisted the neighbors had only hung the sign because they were vacationing. As the boy got ready to dive in, the girl stood on the pool deck. The moon illuminated the pool, and as the boy jumped, she screamed. The light revealed that the pool was empty. It was being repainted while the neighbors were out of town. The sign was hung to keep people safe, not to spoil their fun.

God's Word, his commands, and his will for us to obey are all for our benefit. His warnings and instructions lead us into righteousness and wisdom. If we are obedient to his precepts, we will have blessings and safety under his watchful care.

In what areas do you struggle with obedience? What can you do to change the choices you make?

Compelling

Those who want to make a good impression outwardly
are trying to compel you to be circumcised.
The only reason they do this is to avoid being
persecuted for the cross of Christ.
GALATIANS 6:12 NIV

Have you ever been cornered by a smooth, fast-talking salesperson? The encounter begins with simple conversation, but soon you are being told that your life has been drab and empty without the item he is selling. It doesn't matter if you can't afford it; you can't live without it.

In the early church, there were some who still held fast to Jewish law and believed that those who were not circumcised, should be. They were insistent that this was a necessity, but in truth, they were just trying to avoid opposition from the Jewish opponents of Christianity. In other words, they were looking out for themselves and placed this physical act above the sacrifice of Christ. The apostle Paul opposed this and encouraged the Galatians that the cross was enough. Christ is all sufficient. He defeated the grave and brought salvation. Nothing other than faith in Jesus is needed.

Do you sometimes find yourself trying to do things to make your position in Christ more secure instead of trusting in Christ alone?

Discerning

You know when I sit down and when I get up;
You understand my thought from far away.

PSALM 139:2 NASB

Have you ever thought about what it would be like to have a personal assistant? Someone who anticipates and discerns your very need? They would keep you on schedule, manage your calendar, and pick up your dry cleaning. If you forgot an appointment, your person would remind you. They would even know what you are allergic to, so if anyone sends you a basket of goodies, they can remove the danger.

Did you know that God is aware of where you are and what you are doing at any given moment? Does that give you comfort or great concern? Your every move, every single desire for good or bad—it is all laid bare before him. If we are living a life for Christ, aiming to act in a holy manner, this would make us feel grateful, safe, and protected. If we are living in disobedience, this should make us shudder and tremble. If we truly love Jesus, we will obey him with pure hearts driven by righteous motives.

Can you think of times in your life when you would prefer that God wasn't watching? If so, is it time to deal with that situation?

Cooperative

I say, walk by the Spirit, and you will not gratify the desires of the flesh. For the desires of the flesh are against the Spirit, and the desires of the Spirit are against the flesh, for these are opposed to each other, to keep you from doing the things you want to do.

GALATIANS 5:16-17 ESV

Scripture says that bad company corrupts good character. If you ever had an experience with a naughty playmate as a child, you may have experienced your mother discouraging a playdate with that person again.

Good and evil will never be on the same side. Scripture says that one day, people will call evil good and good evil, but there is no way that the two can ever cooperate with each other. Like the visual of the angel on one shoulder and the devil on the other, we must understand that our flesh and spirit are at war, and we must choose a side. If we want to live like Christ and make an impact for his kingdom, we must deny our flesh and follow the leading of the Holy Spirit in all things. Choose this day whom you will serve. The sooner you put your flesh to death, the sooner you can focus on fulfilling the destiny God has designed for you.

What can you do to more consistently follow the Spirit?

August

In his kindness God called you to share in his
eternal glory by means of Christ Jesus. So after
you have suffered a little while, he will restore,
support, and strengthen you, and he will place
you on a firm foundation.

1 PETER 5:10 NLT

Enlightened

I pray that the eyes of your heart may be enlightened in order that you may know the hope to which he has called you, the riches of his glorious inheritance in his holy people, and his incomparably great power for us who believe.

EPHESIANS 1:18-19 NIV

Can you remember a time in your life where you tried to grasp a concept and it just kept evading you? Maybe you researched and read the intricate information over and over, but it just didn't click. In Ephesians, the apostle Paul wanted to make sure the saints he had ministered to could maintain a firm grasp on what treasures were theirs in Christ. So, he prayed for them. He asked God to open the eyes of their hearts so that, in the depths of their souls, they would understand the wonder of the hope of their calling in Christ.

This hope was their guarantee of eternal life, sealed with the Holy Spirit. For them and us, this inheritance is a promise from God that we are his. His inheritance is the possession of his saints, his chosen people, the bride of Christ. God's Word is full of his glorious instructions. Pray that he will open the eyes of your heart and give you understanding to discern his truth.

Is there a Scripture passage that you have had difficulty understanding? Ask the Holy Spirit to give you the wisdom to understand it.

Flexible

Do all that you can to live in peace with everyone.
ROMANS 12:18 NLT

All of us have had a difference of opinion with someone. Truth be told, we have probably had quite a few! From family to friends to business acquaintances, seeing eye to eye can be like the blind leading the blind. It can cause us to steer clear of any real and vulnerable conversations to avoid conflict. Or we can get riled up, dive in, and end up causing relationship-wrecking division.

God's Word tells us to do all that we can to keep the peace with everyone. This takes colossal self-control. We must be willing to follow Scripture and put others ahead of ourselves, which leads to the question: how would we want to be treated? Golden rule everybody, golden rule. If we adhere to what the Word says, we can bring calm to a heated situation and stay peaceful ourselves. God's peace is best for us and best for others, and the fruit of it preserves our standing with those we care for. They might even see Jesus in us.

When you get into discussions that rub you the wrong way, what is your strategy for maintaining peace?

Poised

Blessed is a man who perseveres under trial; for once he has been approved, he will receive the crown of life which the Lord has promised to those who love Him.

JAMES 1:12 NASB

Have you ever watched the life of someone who seems to get kicked repeatedly when they are down? You wonder, did they do something to bring this on themselves? Or, boy, they just can't catch a break! When someone is bitter about their circumstances, it's difficult to comfort them or help them see things differently. Those that weather the storm well amaze us.

Jesus told us that we would have trouble in this world, so don't be surprised when it comes. If you understand the character of God, it makes trials easier to understand and bear. He promises his love, he promises his protection, and he promises the presence of his Holy Spirit. God even tells us what the result of persevering under trial is, and we would do well to remember it during the onslaught. If we are faithful through trials, our Father promises a crown of life to those who love him. Knowing God is by our side, controlling the outcome of the struggles we encounter, should give us immeasurable peace.

When you encounter difficult situations in life, do you fix them yourself? Or do you place your trust in God?

Favored

The angel went to her and said,
"Greetings, you who are highly favored!
The Lord is with you."

LUKE 1:28 NIV

We all want to be approved of, liked, and accepted. When others ignore or shy away from relationship with us, it hurts. It makes us wonder, is it us or them? It is good to look within and see if there is any offense in us. Maybe our actions weren't quite congenial. Or maybe a relationship just isn't in the cards with that individual, and that's all right. If this is the case and you are hungry for like-minded companionship, pray and ask God to bring the right people into your life.

The account of Mary, the mother of Jesus, makes it clear how God viewed her. She was highly favored, chosen for the great honor of carrying the Son of God. If you wonder how being so favored by God would make you feel, realize if you are in Christ, you are highly favored by God. If you feel drawn to do something big for his kingdom, ask him. God's eyes roam throughout the earth looking for those whose heart is fully his. He is waiting to hear you say, "Here I am. Send me."

Do you truly believe that you are favored by God?

Happiness

*"His master replied, 'Well done, good and faithful
servant! You have been faithful with a few things;
I will put you in charge of many things.
Come and share your master's happiness!'"*

MATTHEW 25:23

What do you think of when you hear the word *happiness*?
Maybe it's the warmth on your face on a sunny day. It might
be an unexpected visit from a good friend or loved one. It can
be recognition of a job well done. It can simply be a smile or
a much-needed hug. Whether we're the recipient or the one
bringing joy, it's balm for our souls.

Happiness can come after a hard time spent on goals, big life
events, or after you have kept your nose to the grindstone and
completed a time-consuming project that thrills your boss. It
shows you are someone to be counted on to do what they say
and bring it to fruition. And if you are known to be a person of
faith, it speaks volumes. If we persevere through this life in what
God asks us to do, we can look forward to the day when we get
to enjoy his happiness. As he welcomes us into his kingdom, we
will hear him say, "Well done, good and faithful servant."

*Do you realize that God sees and is watching your progress,
your attitude, and your faithfulness in the work you do?
Does that change how you might act today?*

Inheritance

"He who overcomes will inherit all this,
and I will be his God and he will be my son."

REVELATION 21:7 NIV

When we receive an inheritance at the result of a loved one's passing, it brings mixed emotions. We would much rather have that person back with us than their items. However, it is comforting to know that we were thought of, and the individual chose what was bequeathed to honor the relationship enjoyed while on this earth.

We can count on every inspired verse in God's Word to be absolute truth. This helps us do all that we can, through the power of the Spirit, to be obedient and keep God's perspective. When we are faced with the consequences of our sins, we must immediately confess, for that is how we overcome. When it is attack from our enemy, we must clothe ourselves with the armor of God to be victorious. When our life is done, God promises that we, as overcomers, will inherit his kingdom and all that comes with it. Most importantly, we will be forever in his presence. He will be our God, and we will be his bride forevermore.

When you encounter difficulties, remind yourself of God's
promises to you. How can you overcome a problem today?

Loyal

O Lord, God of our fathers Abraham, Isaac and Israel,
keep this desire in the hearts of your people forever,
and keep their hearts loyal to you.
1 Chronicles 29:18 NIV

When we give someone a task, we want them to follow our directions and dutifully carry it out. One person might appear eager on the outside while inwardly wondering if they can get away with the bare minimum. Another individual can be proactive, want a great outcome, and give it their all.

When God asks us to do something, most of us are probably thrilled to be chosen and eager to work. But as times passes, we can get distracted and replace what we should be doing with activities that please our flesh. Our heavenly Father only wants what is best for us, and he knows that we will stay steadfast in our faith if our hearts are fully devoted to him. David prayed for God to keep a yearning forever in the hearts of the Israelites to preserve their devotion to God. Jesus wants to keep us close and increase the intimacy we have with him. Set your heart to be faithful, true, and loyal to our Lord.

Where are the areas in your life where you heart tends to go off on its own, forgetting whom it belongs to?

Open

"Listen! I am standing at the door, knocking;
if you hear my voice and open the door,
I will come into you and eat with you, and you with me."

REVELATION 3:20 NRSV

If you have ever lost your keys and locked yourself out of your home, you know how incredibly frustrating it is. You wonder how long it will take to rectify the situation. It certainly won't be as quickly as you would like. Breaking a window or busting down the door suddenly seem like reasonable options.

Jesus stands at the door of our heart, and Scripture advises us to listen, hear his voice and open our heart to him. He is a complete gentleman about it, for he doesn't force his way in. There will be no doors busted or locks picked. He gives us the invitation to surrender and be transformed by the lover of our souls who wants to inhabit our lives. If we make the best decision of all by letting him in, he brings with him forgiveness of sin, the gift of his Holy Spirit, abundant life, his abiding presence, love, his protection, and eternal security. If you have never opened the door of your heart to Jesus, listen closely and you will hear a knock. Let him give you the strength to open the door.

If you don't know Jesus as your Savior, will you receive him today?

Protected

Those who love me, I will deliver;
I will protect those who know my name.
When they call to me, I will answer them;
I will be with them in trouble,
I will rescue them and honor them.

PSALM 91:14-15 NRSV

Have you ever been in a frightening situation that you had hoped to never experience? Maybe your car broke down at night on a dark, desolate road. Perhaps, while trying to get a good night's sleep, you heard the pipes rattling but then believed there was a break-in. Or you are awakened at midnight by a dreaded phone call. Any of these scenarios are scary and stress-inducing.

If you call out to your heavenly Father, he is there immediately with the promise to rescue you and protect you. No matter what the situation is, he will always deliver you. You might be thinking, "But I know people who did not get rescued." How do you know that God didn't show up? His ways are higher than ours, and his thoughts are not our thoughts. He knows and sees things we don't. Whatever the trial, you can be certain God did rescue you, for he is always true to his word. Someday everything will be explained, but for now, just trust and remember he is always faithful.

Do you truly believe that God knows and only does what is best?

Radiant

I prayed to the LORD, and he answered me.
He freed me from all my fears.
Those who look to him for help will be radiant with joy.
PSALM 34:4-5 NLT

Some people love to be scared, so when it is time to choose a movie, they have a one-track mind. Horror films are very popular. People love the ominous music that signals impending doom, and they squeal in a mixture of glee and terror when the strike comes. For them, fear is an emotion to be embraced. Just as many people don't like to be frightened. After a terrifying thriller, they would be in the fetal position for days. Give them a good old G-rated animated film, however, and they are happy as a clam.

For the Christian, fear is an unnecessary experience. A spirit of fear does not come from God; in fact, he wants to free us from all our fears. Fear is an attack of the enemy, but it is our choice to live in tandem with it. If we rebuke fear, it will flee. What we are left with is an exorbitant amount of peace, relief, and radiant joy. Don't choose fear. Choose freedom!

Today, can you find a courageous verse that you can memorize to drive fear from your mind next time it rears its ugly head?

Genuine

These trials will show that your faith is genuine. It is being tested as fire tests and purifies gold—though your faith is far more precious than mere gold. So when your faith remains strong through many trials, it will bring you much praise and glory and honor on the day when Jesus Christ is revealed to the whole world.

1 PETER 1:7 NLT

There are some predicaments in life that astound us. We hear of a tragedy and the mere idea of it shakes us to our very core. It is overwhelming to think that such a thing could happen. And to fathom that anyone could emerge from such a thing, we wonder if it is possible that life for them can ever be the same.

For unbelievers, it can be impossible to believe there is a good reason behind a hardship. As Christians, we know that we encounter trials to refine our convictions. Our faith is so cherished by our Father that he proclaims it more valuable than gold. It pleases him when our faith is proved authentic by withstanding adversity and coming out the other side stronger than before. He promises that once our faith is victorious, we will garner glory, praise, and honor. We will receive these on the day when our precious Lord and Savior, Jesus Christ, is revealed to the entire world.

When trials come and you feel weakened in faith, can you pray about it? Ask God to prepare you to stand firm.

Restored

He restores my soul;
He leads me in the paths of righteousness
for His name's sake.

PSALM 23:3 NKJV

Rest is something we all need, and most of us don't get enough. We toil all day and when we crawl into bed, we are unable to shut our brains off. There are days with multiple appointments, daily demands, and perhaps a new committee to chair or volunteer hours to put in. We place ourselves on the precipice of burnout, saying we will refuel but never getting around to it.

We would do well to heed the example God set for us by taking the seventh day of creation off. God knows full well that if our temples are run down, we will lack energy and passion and instead make poor choices, maybe even unrighteous ones. We never want to give into the enemy's lies that if we do more, we earn more notches on our spiritual belt. We are not saved by works, but by the cross of Christ. God wants us to be discerning and not say yes to every opportunity that is offered to us. Yes, he gives strength, but both God and medical science have spoken; we must take times of rest. Listen to God. When he tells you to take a break, believe him and do it.

If you find yourself anxious, short-tempered, or scatterbrained, when was the last time you truly rested?

Shrewd

"I am sending your out like sheep among wolves.
Therefore, be as shrewd as snakes
and as innocent as doves."
MATTHEW 10:16 NIV

Have you ever encountered someone who knows how to work the art of the deal? An outgoing salesperson greets you enthusiastically, almost like you are a long-lost friend. You feel comfortable, possibly even friendly, with this nice person who must have your best interest at heart. They reel you in, come in for the kill, and you find yourself leaving their place of business in a haze, wondering why you bought an expensive or useless item.

When Jesus sent the disciples out to the surrounding regions, he warned them to be shrewd as snakes but innocent as doves. What does this mean? He wanted them to be wise, respectful, and kind, and he also knew they needed to recognize what was evil. We also need to have the features of a snake and a dove in this world. Scripture encourages us to be alert, watch, know the times we are living in, and react as Jesus would—with wisdom, discernment, and love.

Do you tend to be a serpent, a dove, or a combination of both?
What features are you lacking?

Spontaneous

Worship Christ as Lord of your life.
And if someone asks about your Christian hope,
always be ready to explain it.
1 Peter 3:15 NLT

Can you remember a time when you were in school and not at all prepared for a test? Did you divert your eyes so the teacher wouldn't call on you? Maybe it's a recent project for work, and you slacked off when you should have persevered. It's a horrible feeling with damaging consequences, especially if you were going for that grade point average or wanted to get a promotion.

The Word tells us to be ready to give an answer for our hope in Jesus. More than a test or a job, someone's eternal security is at stake. God has given us ample instruction in Scripture to prepare us. We are to study the Bible, for this discipline helps us learn about him. Then we overflow with joy of who he is and what he has done for us, and we want to shout it from the rooftops. We are to know the Word and have our testimony ready to share at any given moment. If we are obedient and prepped with a response, we will help bring others into his kingdom.

Are you ready to give an answer for your hope in Christ to anyone who asks? What does that answer sound like? Say it out loud.

Tranquil

*The fruit of the Spirit is love, joy, peace, patience,
kindness, goodness, faithfulness, gentleness, self-control;
against such things there is no law.*
GALATIANS 5:22-23 ESV

We live in a rat race of a world. We want everything delivered
at warp speed, from microwaves to finding answers via the
internet faster than we can type the question. We have no idea
of what it is like to wait. This has made us rushed, irritable, and
drained us of a rested mind and tranquility.

The fruit of the Spirit is the answer to our lack of peace. When
we are patient, we don't demand that we get things immediately.
With joy, we aren't so irritable when things don't go our way.
When we have self-control, we don't look aggravated when the
line we are in is deathly slow. If we are kind and have goodness,
we will look to the needs of others ahead of our own. When we
love the Lord and are faithful in following him, we allow his
timing to be our timing. Nothing in the world can compare to
the glorious gifts of the Spirit as we allow him to plant them
into our daily lives.

*If someone asked you which spiritual fruits you have incorporated
into your life, what would you say?*

Unquestionable

Jesus said to him, "I am the way, and the truth, and the life; no one comes to the Father except through Me."

JOHN 14:6 NASB

There are certain things in this world that we expect to stay fixed. We trust these things will be there when we wake up tomorrow morning. We believe our loved ones will be there. We are certain the earth will turn on its axis and life will continue as planned. Of course, nothing is absolute. We have all lost loved ones. The earth will probably continue to spin until God creates his new heaven and earth, but that's no guarantee that life will look the same.

There are some things that will always be constant and true. We cannot earn our salvation. We are sinners who need the Savior. God desperately wants us to become his children and live with him forever in eternity. And there is only one way that we can accomplish all these things. It is solely through Jesus Christ and his provision on the cross. There is no other way, there is no other truth, and there is life only in and through him. If you don't have security in your salvation and your eternal home, won't you surrender to Jesus today?

Have you shared salvation in Christ with anyone lately?

Vigilant

"Watch and pray so that you will not fall into temptation. The spirit is willing, but the body is weak."

MATTHEW 26:41 NIV

Many people have cameras on their front doors. These are linked to their phones so that they have video access to see anyone approaching their home. The goal is to be prepared, ready to react if the individual is up to no good. It's an attempt to protect you from a dreadful intrusion.

We are saved by grace but will continue to face temptation as long as we live on earth. We have an enemy, and he and his dominion are relentless. We also have the Holy Spirit who can overpower any attack that evil may launch against us. But what if we aren't watching for Satan's schemes? We will most certainly be caught unawares and may succumb to the weakness of our flesh. God's Word tells us to watch and pray. It is not so we will fulfill spiritual assignments; it is for our good. The best way to win the battle is to stay aware, and that takes time spent in Scripture and alone with the Savior.

When was the last time you were caught off guard by temptation? How can you prepare for the next time?

Talented

> *"I have filled him with the Spirit of God, with skill,*
> *ability and knowledge in all kinds of crafts."*
>
> EXODUS 31:3 NIV

If you have ever watched an interview with a famous performer who admitted to terrible stage fright, it probably shocked you. You expected the star to be completely comfortable in the spotlight, secure and confident in their talent. You had no idea that they sometimes doubted themselves as you might when faced with a situation where you were insecure about your skill. Approaching a task that we believe is a stretch for us can make us quiver in our boots.

Some things may be impossible for us, but everything is possible with God. When we go to him in humility and ask for help, we can rely on him to fill us, equip us, and provide all that we need through his endless and divine ability. Why should we try to do it on our own? The Creator of the universe is waiting for us to inquire of him so he can bless us through the power of his Holy Spirit.

Can you think of a time when you didn't rely on your own strength or knowledge but instead went to God for help? When do you hesitate to rely on God?

Understanding

*"Call to me and I will answer you and tell you
great and unsearchable things you do not know."*
JEREMIAH 33:3 NIV

Think back to an insightful speech you once heard in college, church, or at a professional presentation. It was probably given by someone you deemed incredibly gifted with superior knowledge and insight. You may have felt lost, like your IQ was a few percentage points lower than the presenter. Still, you were engaged because you wanted to learn and grow in your understanding.

Human knowledge is helpful, and we need it for our daily lives, but nothing can compare to the mind of our God. He clearly says in the Word that our thoughts are not his thoughts. In fact, he tells us that as high as the heavens are above the earth, so are his thoughts higher than our thoughts. He invites us to come to him and hear of great and unsearchable things we do not know. What an amazing invitation! Our heavenly Father, who has infinite knowledge and understanding, wants to share his miraculous insight with us. All we need to do is call on him, and he promises faithfully to answer.

If you have never called on God to seek him for his great and unsearchable thoughts, will you today?

Efficient

The plans of the diligent lead surely to abundance,
but everyone who is hasty comes only to want.
PROVERBS 21:5 NRSV

Can you think back to a time in school when a science project was assigned? You had several weeks to do your best to earn the grade your parents expected of you. You thought you had tons of time, so you procrastinated. Suddenly, it's the week of your presentation and you have no project. You speedily throw something together that will pass. When the night of the science fair comes, there you are with your skimpy project amidst flowing volcanos, electrical gadgets, and your parents' disapproval.

Scripture tells a parable about a master who gave three of his servants some tasks to complete in his absence. Upon his return, one servant was wise and experienced great success, another didn't do as well but resulted in some success, and the third was lazy and did nothing at all. The third was cast out of his master's presence. Now, God wants the best for us. Jesus invites us to abundant life in him, which includes serving as he did. That takes commitment and planning, not last-minute efforts. Let's prepare our hearts and our actions.

Are you a preparer or a procrastinator? Which areas of your life need more diligence?

Accepted

"The Father gives me the people who are mine. Every one of them will come to me, and I will always accept them."

JOHN 6:37 NCV

If you were anxiously waiting to hear if you made the team, were accepted to your first-choice college, or got that dream job, you probably experienced waves of doubt. Every minute on the clock seemed to quadruple in length. You had no guarantee that you would be granted the position you wanted, and there was nothing you could do about it.

God's Word says that no one comes to Jesus unless the Father draws them, and nothing can remove us from him once we do. He loved us before we loved him. He chose us. Jesus, God himself, became man and took our place on the cross and the punishment for our sin. He has redeemed us, transformed us, and given us eternal life. He provides, protects, gives peace, and fights our battles to victory. He is the one shouldering the responsibility for our salvation, and we are invited in freely. Jesus promises to accept all that the Father gives him. There is no greater love, and it is wholly ours.

Have you spent time in worship today? Place your pains and thanksgiving at Jesus' feet.

Adaptable

"You cannot serve both God and money."
MATTHEW 6:24 NIV

We grow up thinking about the kind of life we will have. Maybe we want a career, a family, a big house, and maybe a fancy car and all the luxuries life can offer. We plan our path to achieve those goals, but all too soon, we are working harder to have them than we are finding time to enjoy them. Maintaining riches becomes a harsh and time-consuming task master that we become enslaved to.

We are warned in Scripture about the temptations of money. Wealth is not inherently wrong, but we cannot serve money and still serve God. We are to love the Lord our God with our hearts, souls, and minds, which requires us to steer clear of making money an idol. Jesus advised us to store up treasures in heaven, because all earthy things will one day burn up and pass away. Providing for the needs of others and sharing out of our abundance increases our heavenly bank account. Be wise. Bless God by serving him as a good steward of the finances he has given you.

Have you taken account of how much you have and how often you share?

Caring

> *People were bringing little children to Jesus for him to*
> *place his hands on them, but the disciples rebuked them.*
> *When Jesus saw this, he was indignant. He said to them,*
> *"Let the little children come to me, and do not hinder*
> *them, for the kingdom of God belongs to such as these."*
>
> MARK 10:13-14 NIV

Growing up, we needed support from parental figures. Whether it was a scratch, a fever, or a shoulder to cry on after a teenage breakup, we were comforted by the attention we received. Some of us, however, may have had a mom or dad who didn't show the affection and care we needed. That leaves a deep longing and often emotional scars. The pain of neglect requires healing from our Savior.

Jesus gave us a beautiful picture of how he feels about all children, and that includes his adult children. He would not allow anyone to hinder little ones from coming to him and stated that the kingdom of heaven belonged to them. The arms of our Savior are open wide and will never close to us. We can come to him with the faith of a child, and we will receive everything that we need. Regardless of what kind of earthly parents you had, you have a heavenly father who loves you and will always care for you.

What attributes of God the Father are you most thankful for?

Comfort

The LORD is close to the brokenhearted;
he rescues those whose spirits are crushed.

PSALM 34:18 NLT

Emotional pain can take much longer to recover from than physical pain. We all face issues and events that distress us, but a broken heart can be so devastating that it takes our breath away. Anyone who has experienced such a heartache knows the initial shock, the disbelief, and the sleepless nights that follow. We long for relief, but the memory keeps replaying in our minds.

When God's children suffer heartbreak, he doesn't want them to endure it alone. He wants to rescue us and be close to us in the sorrow. Unfortunately, our discomfort can blind us from remembering the Lord is there, or even make us wonder if he cares. Our enemy takes advantage of our grief by causing us to question God. The truth is, our heavenly Father wants to take our burdens for us. His shoulders are more than able to carry our loads and he cares more for us than any human ever could. Call on him; he will answer, console, and deliver you.

When difficulties arise, do you go to God right away for comfort?
Which ones have you shouldered alone?

Disciplined

Whom the LORD loves He disciplines,
Just as a father disciplines the son in whom he delights.

PROVERBS 3:12 NASB

"Look both ways when you cross the street."
"Don't eat your food so fast."
"Never ever talk to strangers."
"If you do that one more time...!"
Most of us remember similar phrases from childhood. The first three are tools to keep us safe. The fourth carries a warning to quickly address stubborn disobedience. If we did not heed it, it was probably reinforced with swift correction.

As a child, it is hard to believe that one of the most loving things a parent can do is discipline. It is painful at the time, but it is done to save them from agony sooner or later in life. Parents who know the value of discipline and deal it out in love give their offspring instruction that is in their best interest. As God's children, when we sin willfully, he must discipline us. His goal is to transform us into the likeness of his Son. He knows what is best for us. He will refine us, turning his treasured possessions from dross into gold.

When God disciplines you, do you receive it humbly, knowing it is for your good?

Discreet

I, wisdom, dwell together with prudence;
I possess knowledge and discretion.
PROVERBS 8:12 NIV

A secret is carelessly shared with someone who was never intended to hear it. They vow not to pass it on, but they spill it to the first person to cross their path. When that person encounters an acquaintance, details are altered and embellishments added. It sounds like a game of telephone that most of us have played for fun. When it is gossip, not a game, it can have a very damaging outcome.

The Bible says that the tongue is a fire, a world of evil among the parts of the body. This may conjure up a memory of a prayer request that sounded more like a sordid tall tale. Even in a church, amongst those who are commanded to love and consider one another more important than themselves, discretion can be in short supply. We forget to pray for wisdom as stories are shared and cause more harm than good. This is sin and grieves our heavenly Father. Be aware before you speak. Check your motives and discern the motives of others.

Do you enjoy a juicy tidbit, or are you trustworthy? What rumors are swirling around your head? Put them to rest today.

Excellence

Finally, brothers and sisters, whatever is true, whatever is noble, whatever is right, whatever is pure, whatever is lovely, whatever is admirable—if anything is excellent or praiseworthy—think about such things.

PHILIPPIANS 4:8 NIV

We know lots of people with different personalities, qualities, and quirks. Some are outgoing and vivacious, eternal optimists. Others are reserved, keep to themselves, and tend to see the glass as half-empty rather than half-full. The first is a joy to be around but may sometimes wear rosy glasses, tending to be unrealistic. The latter may be full of worry and trepidation that colors every decision they make. One thing is certain: they both have very different mindsets.

Our thoughts affect our actions and attitudes. In Scripture, God tells us how to think. We are to take every thought captive to the throne of Christ. We are to train our minds to dwell on thoughts that represent truth, righteousness, purity, and what is lovely and admirable; things that lead to praise. As we condition our minds to think this way, we can put these qualities and truths into practice. As we focus on these things, incorporating them into our minds and hearts, we will grow into a life of moral and spiritual excellence.

What do you fill your mind with?

Responsible

*"Arise! For this matter is your responsibility,
but we will be with you; be courageous and act."*
EZRA 10:4 NASB

Were you ever part of a school group project where everyone's
grade depended on everyone doing their assigned part?
Or maybe it was a project that required two co-workers to
collaborate on an office presentation. We all know that it
requires commitment and follow-through from all involved.
When that doesn't happen, there are negative feelings. Those
who did the work suffer the same consequences as the ones
who didn't and are left with the bitter taste of unfairness in
their mouths.

God expects his children to be responsible for the work he has
called them to. He promises to fight our battles. We just need
to put on the armor and show up. If we neglect the spiritual
disciplines of prayer and studying his Word, we are neglecting
the things we need to carry out the destiny God has for us. We
are saved by grace, but the way we represent and serve Christ
speaks loudly to our love and commitment to him on this earth.

*Do you act to fulfill all that God asks out of gratitude and love
for what he has done for you?*

Exceptional

*Daniel so distinguished himself among the
administrators and the satraps by his exceptional
qualities that the king planned to set him
over the whole kingdom.*

DANIEL 6:3 NIV

If you want to be known for being truthful, trustworthy, and reliable about your commitments, then you need to exhibit those qualities in your work and social life. People watch, and they make a mental note of the behavior of others. You are known more for your actions than your words. Gaining respect takes consistent modeling of good morals and reliability. These characteristics will open doors of opportunity and give you the authority to speak into others' lives.

When Daniel was brought before the king, it was to be recognized for his insight, intelligence, and outstanding wisdom. There was no one in the kingdom that could rival his excellence. He became so distinguished that even those who were jealous and tried to find something to charge against him failed. What was Daniel's secret? He sought, honored, worshiped, and followed God. He was known for his excellence, and he stood up for what was right, even if it threatened his life. God was always faithful to deliver him.

What will you do to seek to live an excellent life for God?

Guidance

When you turn to the right or when you turn to the left,
your ears shall hear a word behind you, saying,
"This is the way; walk in it."

ISAIAH 30:21 NRSV

If you have ever been lost, you know how desperately you want to get back on the right path. What about the time you made that poor decision? You desperately wish you could turn back time and do it differently. When you are considering an opportunity that affects everything about your future, you wish you had the voice of wisdom to shed light on the right choice.

As a child of the King, you must decide if you will seek and listen to God's will. The Word says that he will tell you which way to go—to the right, to the left, or to just stand still while he fights for you. You don't need to fret or agonize unless you are trying to go your own way and follow your own intentions. Going off and trusting only yourself is a disastrous choice. God has promised never to leave or forsake you, and he wants to direct you to a good and abundant life in him. Are you listening?

How can you better tune your ears to hear God's voice?

Serenity

*The effect of righteousness will be peace
and the result of righteousness,
quietness and trust forever.*

ISAIAH 32:17 NRSV

The soothing sound of a waterfall. The warmth of the sun on a bright summer day. The laughter of a child. The coziness of a cup of tea and a good book on a winter's night. The security of having family and friends you can count on. The satisfaction of being told you have done a good job. All these things bring joy and a sense of peace, but the peace of God is the result of righteousness.

According to Scripture, a righteous man delights in God's law and meditates on it day and night. He prospers in all he does, is morally excellent, and never listens to the advice of the wicked. Yet his Word also says there are none that are righteous, so how will we find peace? The answer is Jesus. When we place our faith in Christ, his righteousness becomes our righteousness because we are filled with his Spirit. Once we belong to Jesus, we are sealed, and nothing can come between us and the promises of our God. Our salvation is sure and our eternity secure. No other truth brings more peace.

Do you believe you are experiencing the fullness of God's peace?

September

My health may fail,
and my spirit may grow weak,
but God remains the strength of my heart;
he is mine forever.

Psalm 73:26 NLT

Provision

*His divine power has given us everything we need for a
godly life through our knowledge of him who called us by
his own glory and goodness.*

2 Peter 1:3 niv

If you found Aladdin's lamp and a genie emerged, you would
have three wishes and could ask for whatever you want.
Depending on your personality, you could wish to control
the world or discover the cure for cancer. Most of us would
probably carefully contemplate all we ever desired in life and
choose carefully. What do we need to request to fill our every
whim and every want?

Our supernatural God knows what we need, and he calls us
to be holy as he is holy. As our good Father, he can supply our
wants if they are asked for with right motives. Through his
power and grace, he has supplied all that is necessary to live a
Christ-like life. He gave us his Word so that we can know his
will and follow his commands. He gave us salvation in Jesus
so that we could be forgiven. We are filled with the fruit of his
Spirit, and if we ask in faith, he will add wisdom, discernment,
knowledge, and understanding. What an extravagant provider!

*Do you utilize the authority and power God has provided you?
What haven't you asked for in prayer?*

Relaxation

Then Jesus said, "Come to me, all of you who are weary and carry heavy burdens, and I will give you rest."
MATTHEW 11:28 NLT

Life can get overwhelming. Unexpected events hit you from out of nowhere, bringing with them added stress and work that you just don't have time for. You exert yourself well past your limit, and you begin to feel like a tiny ant pushing a massive rock up a gigantic hill. You know you need to rest, but you can't fit it into your busy schedule.

Jesus told us we would face troubles on this earth. He knew trials would come that would rest like boulders on our shoulders. He gave us the forewarning but also the solution. We are to bring our worn and weary souls to Christ, who has graciously offered to carry the load for us. We are never to fear or be anxious, for we have an all-powerful Savior who loves us so much that he took the ultimate suffering for us. We should never hesitate to run and hide under the shadow of his wings, allowing him to comfort and lift us up amidst adversity.

When you are exhausted or troubled, do you run to the Savior first or someone else?

Purpose

I know that You can do all things,
And that no plan is impossible for You.
JOB 42:2 NASB

What if you had the power to make everything you do turn out exactly as you desire? You could invent any opportunity and be assured that you would capture it. Let's add superhero powers to the equation. Not only would you meet your goals, but you would do it magically. No one could rival you, and no one could stop you. If you only used your abilities for good, what a wonderful world it would be!

As you envision this, remember who your God is. He is divinely, supernaturally capable of anything and everything. There is no one—not Satan and his demons or any human—who can alter the outcome of his perfect will. The enemy can try to throw a wrench in the plans, but he has no power over God. We can decide to direct our own life and ignore God's leading, but we are the ones who lose. His will is always accomplished, with or without us. If we walk through life with our Savior, nothing is impossible. His plan for us is secure!

Do you trust God's plan for you without question? What areas do you struggle to turn over to God?

Reasonable

*Let your reasonableness be known to everyone. The Lord
is at hand; do not be anxious about anything, but in
everything by prayer and supplication with thanksgiving
let your requests be made known to God.*

PHILIPPIANS 4:5-6 ESV

Some people like to debate while others run from it like the
plague. There are many families who dread holiday gatherings
because they know that a few of their loved ones like to engage
in verbal fisticuffs. If any of your relations are stubborn, you
have no doubt witnessed how difficult it can be to bring them to
a conclusion acceptable to both sides. At the end of the day, no
one has won, and everyone is out of sorts.

God is pleased when we exhibit reasonable behavior. God is
watching us constantly, so why would we want to spin tales
of controversy or dispute things to cause ill will and divide?
We have no reason to be agitated and should get along and
stay at peace with all. We are called to pray, sharing our own
requests and the needs of others with the Lord, full of gratitude
that he hears and answers. Don't waste your time on useless
arguments; be a peacemaker who treats others as Jesus would.

*If someone who knows you was asked to describe your
temperament, what do you think they would say?*

Hardworking

*Let us not grow weary of doing good,
for in due season we will reap,
if we do not give up.*

GALATIANS 6:9 ESV

You have worked harder than you ever have before. You put in overtime and dedicated most waking moments to getting the project done exactly as you desired. The big day comes, and you present it to the boss or committee who commissioned it from you. The big "atta girl" you expected doesn't materialize. Your heart sinks a bit, but you listen to constructive criticism, determined to go back to the drawing board and get it right.

At times, we get weary of trying and want to throw in the towel. God gives us plenty of promises that help us push through. When we are praying for a lost loved one, he doesn't want us to give up, for he is working on their heart. If we are unemployed or sick, he doesn't want us to lose hope, but to praise him in the storm and wait for our miracle. When we are witnessing for him at home or in a foreign land and people are not responding, have faith in his power. Share the gospel, and don't give up!

If things don't turn out as you hoped today, will you lose hope or persevere?

Virtue

*Make every effort to add to your faith goodness; and
to goodness, knowledge; and to knowledge, self-control;
and to self-control, perseverance; and to perseverance,
godliness; and to godliness, mutual affection; and to
mutual affection, love.*

2 PETER 1:5-7 NIV

We have all known at least one person who seemed practically perfect. Always presentable from head to toe, a smile on their face and a pleasant greeting that showed interest in how we were. They are not one to spread rumors and are respectful in their conversation and actions. Their character is constant, and they can be trusted to always keep their word. In short, they are virtuous.

Like the fragrant smell of a beautifully blooming rose, the aroma of Christ wafts through our lives as we serve as the hands, feet, and heart of Jesus, and the world notices. People want to know why you are different. What do you have, and how they can get it? This is a perfect opening to share the love and salvation offered to them by the Savior, who is knocking on the door of their heart. By committing ourselves to grow in Christ toward godliness, we will draw others to him, reflecting him in every aspect of life and fulfilling the great commission.

When people meet you, do they see Jesus?

Worth

You are altogether beautiful, my darling,
beautiful in every way.

Song of Solomon 4:7 NLT

At one time or another, everyone struggles with self-image and value. We live in a society that is appearance-conscious and gives special treatment to those who are beautiful. It is easy to become discouraged or tenaciously competitive. We don't even have to leave home to feel envy for another's lifestyle or appearance. Social media is full of attractive people living fabulous lives that we feel certain we will never achieve.

It's important to remember that God thinks differently than we do. Man looks at the outside, but God looks at the heart. He considers our motives, our praise, worship, and the desire we must put him first. He is the one we must look to for our worth and identity. Consider what the heavenly Father and his Son went through to have you. God watched Jesus brutally mistreated and put to death just so you could come to salvation. He allowed this because to him, you were worth it.

Can you spend time today praising Jesus for what he gave up to gain you?

Stunning

*Let your adorning be the hidden person of the heart
with the imperishable beauty of a gentle and quiet spirit,
which in God's sight is very precious.*

1 PETER 3: 4 ESV

Everywhere we look, we see the world's beauty standards. They can come at a high cost, from clothes to makeup to hair. Popular cosmetic procedures of today can quickly whittle away your savings as you try to emulate the latest magazine cover or social post displaying the most beautiful woman in the world. Comparing can become a vicious cycle of striving for and not achieving perfection. In reality, you are still the same person you were before, and all your efforts didn't bring lasting happiness.

We have all heard the saying that beauty is in the eye of the beholder. Aren't you thankful that the one who matters most, your heavenly Father, sees beyond the outward appearance and considers your heart, first and foremost? As you seek him and the likeness of his Son in your life, he is thrilled as he watches you display a compassion. He finds you exquisite when your thoughts and actions reflect his Son. You are gorgeous to God when your loving spirit attracts people to Christ. Disregard the world's viewpoint and choose to see yourself as Jesus does.

Do you see yourself as God views you?

Reputable

The word of the LORD is right and true;
he is faithful in all he does.

PSALM 33:4 NIV

If you have done business with someone unreputable, no doubt it is a miserable memory. You may have had doubts about the individual, but decided you were just being paranoid and gingerly moved forward. Things seemed to go well for a while, but the day came when you realized you had been deceived. Maybe your money disappeared with the person or they just skipped town, leaving a job or promised possession unfulfilled. You believed a scoundrel and vowed to be smarter next time.

People will disappoint us, and the magnitude of that will vary. There is one, though, who will never fail us. He will never go back on his word or let us down in any way. It is simply impossible for our God to do anything but that which is perfect in every way. He is the same yesterday, today, and forever and we can rely on his righteousness, faithfulness, and salvation. He will always love us, forgive us, help us, and keep his eye on us. He is truth; he is good. We are his and he is ours. Our God never changes!

Can you dwell on who God is today and give praise?

Miraculous

He is your praise; he is your God,
who has done for you these great and awesome things
that your own eyes have seen.
DEUTERONOMY 10:21 NRSV

Fairy tales and superhero epics are resplendent with magic and miraculous deeds of strength and accomplishment. It's a world where nothing is impossible. Even mere mortals who happen into the realm can, if gifted by supreme powers, achieve legendary feats of their own. Alas, these are only stories for entertainment. There are no fairy godmothers, and as much as we would like Superman to come to our rescue, he won't.

But there is our God, truthfully miraculous and all-powerful in everything he says and does. From creation to the parting of the Red Sea, from Jesus' birth to his resurrection, he performs the supernatural regularly. He heals the sick and protects us from harm we don't even see. He oversees and controls the outcome of the spiritual battle with the enemy that is going on in the heavens and on earth, and he is always victorious. There is only one true superhero and his name is Jehovah El-Shaddai—the Lord God Almighty who deserves our praise.

Do you really believe that there are supernatural and miraculous works today?

Resilient

Though the fig tree does not bud and there are no grapes
on the vines, though the olive crop fails, and the fields
produce no food, though there are no sheep in the pen
and no cattle in the stalls, yet I will rejoice in the LORD,
I will be joyful in God my Savior.
HABAKKUK 3: 17-18 NIV

Many people across the world face hunger and try to survive in conditions of poverty daily. Our country has seen a surge of homeless communities, tents strewn through streets and parks. Whether you have suffered lack for an extended period or have recently lost your business or livelihood, it is a challenging situation in which to find yourself. At times like this, hope and gratitude can be in short supply.

Life can be harsh. When it is, we get discouraged and want to know why. We also have a God who asks us to trust him. We don't see the provision that is up ahead, but our Father, who is providing it, does. Regardless of the situation, he is still working on our behalf and is only capable of good. When circumstances are bleak and we have no answers, we can believe he will make a way. Rejoice in who you belong to, find joy in who God is, and live by faith.

When times are tough, do you strive to fix the problem or trust in God? What problems can you turn over to the Father today?

Sincere

We are not, like so many, peddlers of God's word,
but as men of sincerity, as commissioned by God,
in the sight of God we speak in Christ.

2 CORINTHIANS 2:17 ESV

Some folks like to spin tales and tell whoppers. An acquaintance or family member may come to mind. The story starts out as believable, but as the narrator gets deeper in, you begin to find the fantastic account doubtful. It can be in good fun, as long as it is for entertainment and not being presented as authentic.

The Bible is inspired by God. We are warned to treat Scripture with truthfulness and never embellish it in any way. Revelation says that no one is to add to the works of his book or remove any parts of prophecy. If they do, plagues will befall them, and God will take away their part in the book of life. This is extremely serious and should be followed with extreme caution. We must have the utmost respect and care for God's Word. Whether we are sharing Scripture privately or publicly, we must present it accurately. The Word's content was spoken by our almighty God to humankind, and those words are living and sacred.

Do you study God's Word in a way that helps you repeat it truthfully?

Elegant

Charm is deceitful and beauty is passing,
But a woman who fears the LORD, she shall be praised.
PROVERBS 31:30 NKJV

Remember that girl in high school: the beauty queen who led the pack? Everyone followed her, wished they were her, and never crossed her. Just being seen with her upped your popularity score. She attracted boys with a coy smile and a twinkle in her eye, line ready to reel them in, even if she wasn't interested. If you ran into that girl today, you might see an entirely different person. Age might not have been kind to her. She can't get attention with mere flattery anymore; her fan base has disappeared, and her acclaim has plummeted.

God tells us in his Word what he holds in high esteem. He praises the woman who knows and respects him, the one who hides his Word in her heart and speaks truth. He gives favor to his children who put him first. Scripture is clear that the fear of God is the beginning of wisdom. When we have a reverent understanding of the Lord's power and authority, it brings him glory. He lovingly approves of our awe for him.

Have you considered what areas of your life reveal that you accurately fear the Lord?

Driven

I am sure of this, that he who began a good work in you
will bring it to completion at the day of Jesus Christ.

PHILIPPIANS 1:6 ESV

The CEO encouraged his employees to strive for excellence
on a big company project. He wanted them to shoot for the
moon and commit to work, whatever hours or days it took. He
assured them that their efforts would bring great success and
help them hit their goal, even though he would not assist. The
work force didn't quite make the deadline with the assignment
or achieve the expected perfection. He couldn't understand why
they had let him down. Meanwhile, his staff felt they had been
set up for failure.

We have a great promise from our Lord who will never leave
us, forsake us, or let us down. He is always there to hear our
prayers and answer them, giving us the help, healing, or vision,
we need. He will never ask anything of us that he doesn't equip
us to do through the power of his Holy Spirit. He has given us
everything we need to live a life that emulates him and brings
glory to him. We have his guarantee that the work he is doing
in us is good and will be fully accomplished.

Can you identify all the ways God works in and through you?

Ethical

He has told you, mortal one, what is good;
And what does the LORD require of you
But to do justice, to love kindness,
And to walk humbly with your God?

MICAH 6:8 NASB

Have you ever felt like you were in the dark about what was expected of you? It's hard to hit the mark when you don't know where the target is. It can cause you to take the wrong approach, leading to the opposite result of what you desired. If others are affected, you might have to deal with disappointment of the way you handled things. If only someone had given you the exact expectations up front!

The Lord is clear in his Word about what he wants from us. Today's verse lays it out and tells us what is good in God's eyes. We are to engage honestly and in truth with others. When we interact with people, it is with compassion and care. When it comes to us, we are to be charitable and consider others first. Thankfully, our Father doesn't leave our actions to chance but graciously informs us of the character that pleases him. We have assurance of his expectations and can be certain that he will supply what we need to attain them.

Have you thanked God for being clear about what he expects of you? Where would you like to ask for more clarity?

Conscientious

*If others see you with your "superior knowledge"
eating in the temple of an idol, won't they be encouraged
to violate their conscience by eating food that has been
offered to an idol?*

1 CORINTHIANS 8:10 NLT

We are all aware that we are far more affected by the actions of others than their words. Words can have a huge effect on us for good or evil, but when we witness someone do something that influences us, we are tempted to copy them. Copying can end either positively or devastatingly. Bottom line, we need to consider what our behavior can do to others.

As believers in Jesus, the world has an opinion of us. We need to ask ourselves, are we living like salt and light? In the church, are our choices to fulfill our desires creating a stumbling block for our younger sisters and brothers in Christ? We must take stock of what we do. We need to ask ourselves if our temporary decisions are good for us and for the body of Christ as well. Will our actions encourage another's growth in Christ or hinder it? We want to be an example of Jesus, spurring one another on to good deeds.

What things can you eliminate from your life that could be stumbling blocks for others?

Blessed

Never doubt God's mighty power to work in you and
accomplish all this. He will achieve infinitely more than
your greatest request, your most unbelievable dream, and
exceed your wildest imagination! He will outdo them all,
for his miraculous power constantly energizes you.

EPHESIANS 3:20 TPT

Daydream about the most fulfilling, amazing, and satisfying situation you could find yourself in. Would this be a vacation with loved ones on a tropical isle, palm trees swaying, sun sparkling on a rolling ocean? Imagine it's an award you are receiving for a job well done, accompanied by an extravagant party in your honor. Or it could be a clean bill of health that includes an approval to go and freely live your life after a long struggle with illness. In any of these scenarios, you have been given something wonderful, and you feel empowered and blessed.

Even if you could envision a life beyond your perfect dream come true, it would never come close to what God has to offer. His perfect plans, gifts, and strength working through us are nothing our minds or hearts could never conceive. His power, which is available to us, is far beyond our capabilities. He does these things out of his great love for us. He deserves our constant worship, gratitude, and songs of thankfulness, today and throughout eternity. He is the only true God worthy of honor, glory, and praise.

What marvelous provisions in your life can you thank God for?

Certain

*Faith is confidence in what we hope for
and assurance about what we do not see.*

HEBREWS 11:1 NIV

What if you could be certain that you could obtain the thing you desire? You daydream that the new talent you are dedicating yourself to will bring you fulfillment and receive accolades from others. You want to believe that a new relationship is strong enough to last, and you trust it won't drift apart. You visualize the thing you are hoping for happening exactly as you want it to.

Giving our hearts to Jesus as our Lord carries absolutes. We're guaranteed that once we accept him as our Savior, we're forgiven all our sins, are new creations, and will live eternally with him. We become filled with his Holy Spirit and endowed with his power. We can accomplish things that are beyond our abilities and comprehension because he is at work within us. But when we doubt his strength at work in us, we shrink back, and we lose the blessing of what happens when we step out in faith. Don't miss his best by losing trust. Know with certainly that you can count on his promises.

Do you trust your Lord consistently and entirely?

Cherished

See how very much our Father loves us,
for he calls us his children,
and that is what we are!

1 JOHN 3:1 NLT

You have great adoration for that special friend or person in your life. Close your eyes and envision them, seeing through your mind's eye. Realize how your world brightens when they are present. Your smile becomes bigger, and your laugh gets louder. You hold the relationship very dear, and you protect it and nurture it so that it endures until the end of time.

This is how our heavenly Father feels about us, only in a more extravagant and holy way. His great love was demonstrated when he gave his one and only Son in exchange for us. Can you even fathom giving the most cherished person in your life for another? God's gift to us is the greatest, most outrageous sacrifice of all time. He did it because he cares so intensely for us. He delights in us. He sings over us. He waits patiently to hear our prayers and listens joyfully as we sing his praise. We are loved beautifully and beyond comprehension by our faithful Abba.

Will you bask in the glow of God's love for you today?

Accountability

Confess your sins to one another and pray for one another, that you may be healed. The prayer of a righteous person has great power as it is working.

JAMES 5:16 ESV

The crime was committed in the dark where no eyes could witness it. When daylight revealed the act, it was unthinkable that someone could conceive of and carry out such a thing. What led this person to do this? Were they mistreated as a child? Did they grow up wild with no understanding of right or wrong? You wonder how this atrocity was even thought of and what type of mind births such corruption.

Most of us will never commit a heinous crime, but God wants us to share our sin with one another as a precaution against repeating the offense. If we speak it, we can't hide it any longer. Instead of harboring something and going deeper into transgression, we open ourselves up to supportive wisdom from a confidant. Confession is good for the soul and sets us free. An accountability partner gives us better chances for overcoming the sin that besets us. A mature friend in Christ understands that we are all capable of wrongdoing and that the best deterrent to bear one another's burdens and lovingly call out evil.

Do you have an accountability partner? If not, will you get one?

Assertive

*Having such a hope,
we use great boldness in our speech.*

2 CORINTHIANS 3:12 NASB

Have you ever known someone who communicates efficiently and bluntly? They do not mince words, and if not presented with tact, their words can wound someone and cause offense. For example, maybe you are seeking counsel. It is in your interest for that person to transfer the information truthfully and with authority, but also with compassion.

In carrying out the great commission, we have a responsibility to present our faith accurately and courageously in love. We must know the Word and present the gospel unapologetically, proving that we are faithful followers who are not ashamed of the gospel of Christ. We may witness to people who will hear about Jesus from no one else. If we don't share, we are hoarding the truth that can save their soul from hell. If you had the cure for cancer, you wouldn't bury it. Why do we hesitate to tell others of the greatest hope there is? Be brave in sharing the gift of God that leads to redemption.

Do you worry about what others think of your faith?

Cognizant

If we confess our sins, he is faithful and just to forgive us
our sins and to cleanse us from all unrighteousness.
1 JOHN 1:9 ESV

Some people are very methodical about making sure they remember things. They make lists, mark calendars, and keep a record of all their appointments and meetings in their phone. Others tend to fly by the seat of their pants, storing information in their head and trusting they will remember. If the latter is a busy person, they are prone to forget and miss important dates.

We may be saved and forgiven, but we do encounter temptation and we still sin. The most important key is to be cognizant that God has given us directions on what to do when we transgress. We are to come to him in prayer, humbly and with a repentant heart, asking forgiveness when we recognize our wrongdoing. He promises he will forgive our sin, forgetting it as if he were casting it to the bottom of the ocean. Sin temporarily breaks our fellowship with God. We must be aware of when we sin and immediately go to his throne of grace and mercy to confess.

When you sin, do you hesitate? Or do you immediately run to Jesus to confess and receive forgiveness?

Alive

> *"Just as the Father raises the dead and gives them life,*
> *so also the Son gives life to those he wants to."*
>
> JOHN 5:21 NCV

Life can seem monotonous at times. Doing the same tasks, day after day, can wear on us. We crave the feeling of something new, something that makes our spirits soar. When you find that experience it can make you giddy, feeling more alive than ever before.

Life is a gift from God, and we all hope for a long one. Still, death is inevitable and will come to all of us. For those in Christ, death is not the end but the beginning. We know that we have eternal life because of Jesus. This miraculous promise breathes life into our souls and helps us quell any fear of the hereafter. When we understand the truth that we were chosen by God before the foundation of the world and our spiritual security has more to do with him than us, it humbles us and fills us with gratitude. In Christ, we are saved, we are sealed, and we will raise from the dead and live with him forever.

How can you express your gratitude to God today that he chose you and will raise you for eternity?

Comfortable

Even though I walk through the darkest valley,
I will fear no evil, for you are with me;
your rod and your staff, they comfort me.

PSALM 23:4 NIV

We all want to be protected and experience well-being, yet we are aware that life can change drastically or end in a heartbeat. The moment we are born, life places us in the shadow of death, eventually arriving at its conclusion. We can be afraid, or we can have peace in knowing that our lives and mortality are in the hands of someone far greater. Our God has given us the option of eternal security with him.

We have a good shepherd who is with us before birth and throughout our entire lives, to our death, and into eternity. As we travel through this earthly sojourn, he is alongside us to guide us, protect us, and correct us if needed. When we stray, he uses gentle but firm discipline to get us back on track, comforting us with his love through the process. He quiets any fear, knowing we need not suffer it. He is controlling the outcome in his perfect will. He is with us, and that is an enormous blessing!

Does death frighten you? If so, why?

Acknowledged

"Whoever acknowledges me before others, I will also acknowledge them before my Father in heaven."
MATTHEW 10:32 NIV

Have you ever been at a party where the host is making introductions and when it comes to you, your name slips their mind? It is embarrassing. No one likes to be forgotten. It does not have to cause an offense, yet you worry that possibly you were an afterthought, or that the host was pressured to include you, someone they don't even remember.

Someday, we will all stand before the Father, and he will open the book of life. The ultimate lack of acknowledgement would be if Jesus turned to the Father and said, looking at you, "This one is not mine. Depart from me; I never knew you." At that point, it will be too late. You no longer have the option to explain your decision to neglect accepting the Savior during your earthly life. You won't be able to excuse not speaking his glorious name to win others to him. The die will be cast. But today, you have time. You have a choice. Choose to align yourself with the name and life of Jesus, and he will do the same for you.

Who can you share salvation in Jesus with today?

Confirmed

If we are faithless, he remains faithful—
for he cannot deny himself.
2 TIMOTHY 2:13 ESV

Sometimes, we hear people saying outrageous things or telling tall tales, and we do not believe them. This can lead to disagreements and broken relationships. Some say that we should never discuss religion or politics, but regardless of what the subject is, we hope a difference of opinion will not sever a friendship.

Jesus had a difference of opinion with the Pharisees. It didn't mean he withheld his love from them. He had sharp retorts for them and tried to instill his teaching, but they held tightly to their own ways, believing they were correct. Their rigidness to believe their own truth instead of his led them to plot his death. They denied him, but he did not deny them. If they had turned, repented, and followed him, he would have welcomed them with open arms. Jesus will never alter his representation of himself as Savior of the world, the only way to the Father. He will always be the only way, truth, and life.

Do you stand in full agreement with all of what Jesus spoke?

Competent

Make every effort to give yourself to God as the kind of person he will approve. Be a worker who is not ashamed and who uses the true teaching in the right way.

2 TIMOTHY 2:15 NCV

The calculus teacher steps to the front of the class and announces the commencement of today's lesson. It will be intellectually challenging, he warns, and it therefore requires the intense focus of the student. The participant will need to listen carefully, thinking critically to begin to understand. The instructor looks at the class and announces, "I want you to comprehend that two plus two is five." Thinking the teacher out of his mind, some choose to agree to protect their grade.

When we study the Word, picking and choosing parts of verses so that it supports what we want instead of reading it in context, affects the meaning. We should study God's Word from beginning to end and within the structure it is written. We cannot effectively present God's Word if we study it incorrectly. There are commentaries, Scripture notes, and of course, the Holy Spirit, to help us when needed. This is the most important subject we can apply ourselves to, and we must do it responsibly.

What portions of God's Word have you neglected to study?

Encouraged

I am convinced that neither death, nor life, nor angels,
nor principalities, nor things present, nor things to come,
nor powers, nor height, nor depth, nor any other created
thing will be able to separate us from the love of God that
is in Christ Jesus our Lord.
ROMANS 8:38-39 NASB

You have entered into an agreement with an individual or a corporation. Everyone is happy, believing this is just the start of a fruitful and lengthy relationship. You have a like-minded goal, and you agree on how to approach it and conquer it. Then, one day, there is a parting of the minds, which leads to a heated discussion and the dissolving of the partnership. Something intended to hold together has fallen apart.

When we come to Christ sincerely, offering our heart and life to him, we are sealed. There is nothing that will detach us from the Savior who now resides within us. We have been filled with the Holy Spirit, who is our constant companion. When the enemy strikes, it may throw us off, but he will not defeat us. Not even death can tear us out of the arms of Jesus. What a glorious truth to know that no matter what, we will always be saved, always be loved, always be protected, and always be watched by the lover of our souls. Praise to our Lord and Savior, Jesus Christ!

Where does your bond with Christ need strengthening?

Active

As we pray to our God and Father about you, we think of your faithful work, your loving deeds, and the enduring hope you have because of our Lord Jesus Christ.

1 THESSALONIANS 1:3 NLT

Everyone needs a support team. If you have ever heard a speech honoring "the woman behind the man," that woman is the one cheering and assisting the man in whatever task was set before him. Another example is the supporting actor role. When that actor earns an award, it means that their work positively helped the lead actor's role.

Recognition and the support of others brings encouragement. Being a prayer warrior for another is one of the greatest gifts we can offer a brother or sister in Christ. When we approach the throne of grace for someone else, it gives that person peace and hope. It can inspire them in times of difficulty, helping them to push through and overcome. When we acknowledge the service and love that another believer provides, we are ultimately giving recognition and praise to Jesus, for it is he who empowers and equips them in their actions. It is God's will that we pray, uphold, and spur others on to good works in his name.

Have you lifted someone up recently by acknowledging their good works in the name of Jesus? Who could use some recognition today?

Cheerful

Let each one give as he purposes in his heart, not
grudgingly or of necessity; for God loves a cheerful giver.
2 CORINTHIANS 9:7 NKJV

Isn't it fun to give someone you care for a gift? You think long
and hard about what they would like before deciding, gleefully
picturing what their face will look like when they open it. When
you remember someone by giving them a thoughtful gift, the
joy is vastly meaningful. You didn't have to do it, but you did
it out of love for that person, and the recipient can feel the
warmth of that affection.

When we give our tithes or service to the Lord with
cheerfulness, it brings him immense joy. If we bring our gifts
resentfully, it saddens him. He loves watching us give back
to him what he gave to us, but only when it comes from an
attitude of gratitude, delivered sacrificially and with happiness.
It is a valuable way to show our appreciation, and it is actually a
kindness that God allows us to present our offerings to him. He
doesn't need them; he is all-powerful and owns everything that
exists. However, it is a way we can please him and show him
how intensely we love him.

Are you a cheerful giver or a reluctant one? What can you happily
give today?

October

I can do everything through Christ,
who gives me strength.

PHILIPPIANS 4:13 NLT

Enriched

Jesus, looking at the man, loved him and said, "There is one more thing you need to do. Go and sell everything you have, and give the money to the poor, and you will have treasure in heaven. Then come and follow me."

MARK 10:21 NCV

If you have ever known a penny-pincher, you know that they are frugal or stingy with their money. Even some millionaires and billionaires reportedly hang on to every cent and don't use their money in any way to help others in need. They hoard every dollar, never sharing with anyone else, and when they die, another gets it anyway.

Jesus knew the heart of the rich man, who valued his wealth and guarded it earnestly. When he ran up to Jesus and inquired how to receive eternal life, the Savior told him to keep the commandments. He replied he had done that since childhood. Jesus responded, "there is one thing you lack." He proceeded to tell the man to give to the poor and place his treasure in heaven, then follow him. Jesus loved the rich man, but the man loved his money more. He couldn't do it. As the rich man walked away, Jesus said, "How hard it is for a rich man to enter God's kingdom." We must serve and follow God, not money.

Is your treasure on earth or in heaven?

Forgiveness

He has delivered us from the domain of darkness and transferred us to the kingdom of his beloved Son, in whom we have redemption, the forgiveness of sins.

COLOSSIANS 1:13-14 ESV

Whether you are one who needs to forgive or desires forgiveness, it can be something you want to avoid. If you have been hurt or are the one who caused the offense, it can be easier to keep quiet instead of humbling yourself and addressing it. Either party can move forward in compassion and want to restore the relationship, but there is no guarantee that they will be accepted.

When we come to Jesus, asking him to save us and forgive our sins, he never has a moment's hesitation. The Word says that God wants every person he created to come to repentance. We are assured that if we confess our sins, he is faithful and just to forgive our sins and cleanse us from all—yes, all—unrighteousness. Were it not for the extravagant grace of God, we would be left to our own devices, and we are unable to save ourselves from eternal doom. His goodness liberated us from the destruction of our souls and made us permanent residents of his heavenly kingdom.

If an offense exists between you and another, will you make peace with them today?

Goodness

Let no corrupt word proceed out of your mouth,
but what is good for necessary edification,
that it may impart grace to the hearers.

EPHESIANS 4:29 NKJV

You peruse your favorite streaming network to find a film that will be appropriate for all ages. It's family movie night, and you want everyone to enjoy the movie. The family settles in, and everything is going well until a coarse word flies out of an actor's mouth, making everyone cringe. You immediately regret your choice. Everyone is aghast as a young one repeats the word loudly and asks what it means. You awkwardly ask, "When did PG include that language?" Grandma may suggest someone else choose the entertainment in the future, giving you a disapproving look.

Scriptures tells us to speak words that edify. There is no place for the Christian to indulge in risqué jokes, foul language, or unseemly discourse. We are to choose our words carefully, always aiming to represent Jesus well. Our speech should lift others up, bringing healing and peace, encouragement, and inspiration. Our conversations should move our brothers and sisters in Christ to thankfulness and worship of God, not make them stumble. We are witnesses in everything we say and do, and the world is watching our behavior.

Have you slipped into a habit of inappropriate speech or language?

Helpful

> "I will ask the Father, and he will give you another
> Helper, to be with you forever, even the Spirit of truth,
> whom the world cannot receive, because it neither sees
> him nor knows him. You know him, for he dwells with
> you and will be in you."
>
> JOHN 14:16-17 ESV

Difficulties come in all sizes and varieties. They are computer issues, plumbing problems, or a broken-down car on the roadside. Maybe it's not a struggle with a material object but a job loss or a broken heart. Whatever we encounter, there are times where we desperately need someone to assist us. If we are counting on the world to provide help, we will often be sorely disappointed.

God's Word says to bring our every need to him; nothing is too big or too small. Jesus knew that when he left this earth, we would need guidance and assurance, and he had a glorious plan to guarantee our inheritance in him. When Jesus ascended, he said the Holy Spirit would come reside with us, guiding us into all truth. The Spirit speaks only what the Father proclaims, giving us wisdom and knowledge. We are filled with his fruit and find that good works are the overflow. We know the Holy Spirit intimately, for he is always in us and with us.

How does it make you feel to know the Holy Spirit dwells in you?

Insightful

Think about what I am saying.
The Lord will help you understand all these things.

2 TIMOTHY 2:7 NLT

When you study a complex subject, you know that your experience can go one of two ways. You might understand it completely right from the start, or you may be totally in the dark for the entire course. You read the information repeatedly, but it's all Greek to you. You are lost and need help to grasp the beginning concepts. If the instructor is unwilling and makes you tough it out on your own, you can hit a mental block wall.

We have a God who invites us to bring anything we don't comprehend directly before his throne. He will never tell us to figure it out on our own; he will equip us with wisdom and knowledge if we ask in faith. He loves to hear from his children and is faithful to endow us with his insight. He wants us to intimately know him and his ways. He eagerly waits for us to sit at his feet and learn from him.

When was the last time you sat in the presence of God, waiting for him to speak?

Gifted

*Every good action and every perfect gift is from God.
These good gifts come down from the Creator of the sun,
moon, and stars, who does not change like
their shifting shadows.*

JAMES 1:17 NCV

Isn't it wonderful when things go exactly as you wish? Life just hums along, and you feel like you have been blessed exponentially. You think you must be living correctly or have incredible favor. People like you, your relationships with friends and family are going splendidly, and life as you know it is fabulous. Then a thought crosses your mind; how long can this last?

As believers in Christ, we are promised that we have a good father who desires to give good gifts to his children. Since we know that God's character is forever unaltered, we know his longing to bestow his best on us will never change. Anything good that happens in our lives is from him. His actions toward us are always done in our best interests and align with his perfect will for us. When life is not going well by our estimation, it is because we can't see what God sees. He wants us to grow in Christ, so sometimes his gifts come wrapped in trials. However, we can be certain that all he does is because he loves us.

Whether it's a good gift or a trial, do you trust God?

Justice

When justice is done, it is a joy to the righteous
but terror to evildoers.

PROVERBS 21:15 ESV

The news station reports that the case trial has begun. The defending attorney and the one who committed the crime have carefully crafted a defense that they hope will twist the framework of justice. They unashamedly present their tainted argument. The verdict is in and the jury has spoken. If justice has been served, those in the right will rejoice as the one who perpetrated the evil shakes in their boots.

Scripture states that it is a fearful thing to fall into the hands of the living God. Those who will stand before God in judgment after defiantly rejecting him will experience extreme horror. They will realize the time to come to salvation has passed. The gavel will fall on eternal separation from God. For those who have received salvation in Christ, it will be a time of rejoicing, celebration, and the start of eternal life in the presence of the Lord. If you are unsure, secure your stance in Jesus today by receiving him as your Lord and Savior.

We have no guarantees of tomorrow. Are you ready to stand before God?

Persistent

"Everyone who asks will receive.
The one who searches will find.
And everyone who knocks will have the door opened."

LUKE 11:10 NCV

The traveling salesman had high hopes that no doors would slam in his face today. His biggest goal was that people would forget to look through the peep hole and instead open the door and give him a chance. It was like looking for a needle in a haystack to find someone who'd allow him to begin his presentation and make it halfway through. If someone allowed him to finish his pitch, it was a good day. If he captured an order, it was cause for celebration.

Jesus has given humanity an extravagant gift. If we ask, we will receive. If we have questions about God, we are invited to seek him, and he promises we will find him. If we have needs, we are told to ask in the name of Jesus and he will meet them. If we approach and want to enter the door of salvation, Christ promises that the door will be opened to us, his blood cleansing us from all sin. He is an enormously generous God who can be counted on. He will never deny those who come to him.

How have you seen God provide for you lately?

Engaging

Your word I have hidden in my heart,
that I might not sin against you.

PSALM 119:11 NKJV

Have you ever passed a driver's test only to leave the premises and forget the laws? You learned enough to get through it successfully and then went back to your ways of navigating the road. Suddenly, you are pulled over by a policeman for irresponsible driving. You try to coerce him out of a ticket with a sob story, embellishing with tears. You would do better to value the law and commit it to memory. If so, you might have remembered that you can't just roll through a stop sign!

When God asks us to commit his Word to memory, it isn't to earn a star on a heavenly report card. It is because he knows that focusing on his Word and reviewing it in our minds will make it part of us. Then, we can easily bring those truths we have memorized to mind when we need a reminder not to sin. When faced with the living Word of God as a deterrent, we have a much greater chance of incorporating it as a weapon against transgression.

Do you memorize Scripture as a regular habit? What verse would you like to start memorizing?

Comprehensive

*I pray that your love will overflow more and more,
and that you will keep on growing in knowledge and
understanding. For I want you to understand what really
matters, so that you may live pure and blameless lives
until the day of Christ's return.*

PHILIPPIANS 1:9-10 NLT

You began a relationship with someone who seemed sincere
and trustworthy. They assured you that they didn't want
anything but your friendship. You trusted them only to find out
that this person had an ulterior motive. They didn't want to be
friends with you as much as they wanted the connection for an
introduction to someone who would benefit them. You learned
a hard lesson about discernment.

Today's verse says that love must overflow more and more, but
it also says to grow in knowledge and understanding about our
hearts' affections. We need to be perceptive when cultivating
intimate friendships. What if a companion who doesn't have
the beliefs we do tries to divert us to activities that are not the
best for us? Bad company corrupts good character, and we can
become gradually influenced for the worse if we are not wise.
We must be committed to living an unadulterated life that is
above reproach, and we are to do so faithfully as we anticipate
our Lord's return.

*Is there anyone in your life that influences you away from
representing Jesus?*

Approachable

O God in Zion, to you even silence is praise!
You who answers prayer;
all of humanity comes before you with their requests.
PSALM 65:2 TPT

You have hit a bump in the road and you really need a favor. You dither about who to go to. You have friends that you could approach and family members who would step in, but they would ask, "How did you get yourself into this mess?" They may agree to give you some support but also lecture you about what you might have done differently. They suggest that you need assistance in this area and should get some help. You say thank you, but you walk away feeling small.

We never need to be concerned about coming to God with any request. We don't have to stress over whether he will listen or think our need is silly. We will never be turned away; he welcomes us with open arms. He loves to hear our voices and he wants to give us our hearts' desires. He is always ready with an answer for those who call on his magnificent name. If you have not been spending time on your knees in prayer, consider the privilege you have been given to boldly approach the throne of God.

Do you prioritize prayer? Where can you add more prayer to your day?

Committed

Devote yourselves completely to the Lord our God,
walking in his statutes and keeping his commandments,
as at this day.

1 Kings 9:1 nrsv

Giving your all to something takes thorough dedication. Imagine you are training for your first marathon. You have never done one before, but it is on your bucket list and there is no time like the present. You vow that you won't miss a single day of training. You research the best exercises and nutrition and pledge to yourself that you will run a little farther each day. You are confident that when the day of the race arrives, you will be a real contender. You run the race and prove that your hard work paid off!

Completing an endurance run is an accomplishment, but running our race well on earth for Jesus is the greatest thing we can achieve. It takes devotion to spiritual disciplines like prayer, studying Scripture, and pursuing God on a daily, consistent basis. We can't expect to grow in our walk with Christ if we don't put the time in. If our hearts are truly devoted to him, it will be our top priority and most treasured pastime.

Do you approach time with God as something to check off your list? Or do you crave time with Jesus?

Enthusiasm

In all the work you are doing, work the best you can.
Work as if you were doing it for the Lord, not for people.
COLOSSIANS 3:23 NCV

When we are facing a task that someone entrusted to us, we have a choice about our work ethic. We can start off empowered, ready to hit the ground running. If the duty is difficult, we can be discouraged from the get-go and wish we could delegate it to another. If we find out it is a lot more difficult than we expected, we can start to lose interest and work just to get it done and over with.

One way we can avoid a negative attitude about a project is to remember that ultimately, we are doing it for God, not a person. He sees everything about us, from our outward manners to the depths of our hearts. He knows what we are going to say before the word is on our lips. If we treat everything we say and do as a testimony of who we are in Christ, seeking to glorify our Lord, we will approach all of life responsibly and with righteous motives.

Does your work show you are serving God?

Admiration

*"Very truly, I tell you, the Son can do nothing on his own,
but only what he sees the Father doing; for whatever the
Father does, the Son does likewise. The Father loves the Son
and shows him all that he himself is doing; and he will show
him greater works than these, so that you will be astonished."*

JOHN 5:19-20 NRSV

Everyone is intrigued when a magician performs unexplainable
illusions. Eyes glued to the stage, the audience exclaims, "That's
amazing! How does he do that?" However, they know that he
would never share his secrets. One mind-boggling trick after
another, each more mystifying than the one before, shifts the
viewers into genuine believers. They exit the show convinced that
this mere human has extraordinary abilities that baffle the mind.

When Jesus left heaven to come to earth as a man on our
behalf, he came as the Word made flesh, filled with the power
of his heavenly Father. In this relationship, there were no
secrets between the Father and the Son. God revealed to his Son
the miraculous works he would do: making water into wine,
healing the sick, raising the dead. People were amazed as they
witnessed these things; some rightly recognized him as the
Messiah. In his final earthly act, Jesus destroyed the grave and
ascended into heaven, leaving the Holy Spirit as our comforter
until his return. This is a mystery made fully known to us so
that we could be saved.

How have the Father and Son worked together on your behalf?

Considerate

Do nothing from selfish ambition or conceit,
but in humility regard others as better than yourselves.
Let each of you look not to your own interests,
but to the interests of others.

PHILIPPIANS 2:3-4 NRSV

If there are children in your life—whether your own, a niece or nephew, or a close friend's offspring—you have probably had to remind that little one to share. It is not in our nature to let someone else go first in line, give someone else the better seat at an event, or bypass the last piece of pie in honor of another. We have a survival instinct that places us in the preeminent spot, even if it only applies to dessert.

The humble, sacrificial act of the cross is the ultimate example of looking to the interests of others ahead of your own. Jesus had every right to stay on the throne and leave us to suffer what we deserved, the penalty of death for our sins. Yet he didn't give it a second thought, He took on the nature of a servant, made in human likeness, and became obedient to take our place and die on Calvary. We are called to have the same mindset as Christ, loving as he loved.

Is it natural for you to put others' interests above your own? Who can you lift up today?

Established

Walk in Him, having been firmly rooted and now being built up in Him and established in your faith, just as you were instructed, and overflowing with gratitude.

COLOSSIANS 2:6-7 NASB

The windstorm was intense, destroying nearly everything in its path. Debris filled the streets as shingles blew off roofs. People ran for cover to avoid being hit by falling tree limbs. If not for basements, many might have sustained injuries that could have been life-threatening. However, one tree in the middle of town was unaffected. Its owner had nurtured it from a sapling, carefully attending to its health and increase. The roots had grown strong and sturdy, extending deep into the ground. No one yelled timber, for the old tree was solidly attached.

Jesus instructs us in his Word to stay connected to him, the vine, as his branches. When we walk with him, commune with him, and grow stronger in our beliefs through faith, it helps us bear fruit in his name. In him, nothing is impossible for us. As we figuratively sit at his feet by reading his Word daily, we mature in knowledge. We trust him with a faith that is unwavering because we understand his character, power, and great love for us. We overflow with joy because we walk closely with the lover of our souls.

Is your faith built solidly on Jesus?

Praise

> *Let everything that has breath*
> *praise the LORD.*
> *Praise the LORD.*
>
> PSALM 150:6 ESV

Everyone jumped to their feet and the audience erupted in applause as the play came to an end. The actors returned to the stage as the audience continued to cheer. Shouts of "Encore!" filled the theater. As the final bows were taken, the players' faces beamed with appreciation for the packed house and the adulation.

We acknowledge the talents and work of others, but the most deserving of our praise is Jehovah El-Shaddai, the Lord God Almighty. Praise is an act that should be in our hearts, minds, and on our lips continually. He alone is worthy. He is the one who gives us breath every day. His plan of salvation saves us from eternal destruction. As we lift our voices in gratitude, prayer, and song, he is intently listening, and it brings him joy. God is enthroned upon our praises as we extol him, proclaim our faith, and give him glory. Someday, even those who have not believed will bow the knee, finally recognizing he is the only true God. All of creation will know and be accountable.

Do your prayers consist more of requests or praise to the Father?

Refined

*Do not lie to one another, seeing that you have put off the
old self with its practices and have put on the new self,
which is being renewed in knowledge after the image
of its creator.*

COLOSSIANS 3:9-10 ESV

The child insisted that he that he hadn't eaten the cookie. He
knew he wasn't supposed to get one on his own or eat it before
lunch. His mother said she was going to ask him one more time
because he had disobeyed in the past and she needed to know
if he had learned his lesson yet. He cried out, "I am telling the
truth!" His mother countered, "Then why is there chocolate on
your face?"

Sometimes we are reluctant to part with certain sins. The Bible
tells us that sin is pleasurable for a season but leads to death.
We promise ourselves each time is the last time, but then the
temptation comes again, and we falter. Scripture says to confess
our wrongs to one another, but we don't want to be judged.
Instead, we deceive. We need to believe that our old ways were
abolished when we accepted Jesus. He makes us a new creation.
If the enemy brings up those old behaviors, be empowered by
the Spirit to shut him down. Remember, we are being renewed
daily in the image of our Savior.

Is there a sin you are giving in to?

Sanctified

"Sanctify them in the truth;
Your word is truth."

JOHN 17:17 NASB

As the athlete spent another day training vigorously for her next competition, a janitor for the stadium watched with a quizzical expression. The competitor noticed the questioning glance but kept her focus on the task at hand. When the onlooker shouted out the question, the professional was ready with an answer. "Don't you get tired of training the same way day after day?" the man asked. "No," she answered. "I know I have been set apart to win."

As believers, we are a special people who are anointed by God. We are not of this world; we are running a race toward the one we belong to. We know that the truthful Word tells us exactly who we are. We are his, adopted through Jesus as the children of God. He chose us before the foundation of the world. We have redemption through the Savior's blood because of God's amazing grace. We have been sealed with the Holy Spirit who guides us and equips us. We were made for his pleasure and have been showered with his love. He has given us spiritual victory in Christ.

Do you share your position in Christ with others?

Skilled

David shepherded them with integrity of heart;
with skillful hands he led them.
PSALM 78:72 NIV

The glass blower attracted a crowd as he expertly brought his work to life. He worked delicately to create art out of formless glass, from small figurines to horse drawn carriages to exquisite castles. The audience conversed with one another, commenting on the intricate skill of the artist as he designed each item with love.

David was known as a man after God's own heart and as a king who presided with great aptitude and virtue. Even though he succumbed to sin in his private life, when he confessed, God treated him as he does all of us. He forgave him and continued to use him to accomplish his will. From the time David faced Goliath to his days on the throne, the Lord equipped him with abilities and expertise. Choosing him when he was a lowly shepherd boy, he raised him to greatness in the service of God. With Jesus, any of us can be used for God's glory if we surrender. Let us allow the greatest craftsman of all to fill us with his power. Absolutely nothing is impossible with God.

Have you allowed God to do anything in and with your life?

Vital

*The Lord God formed the man of dust from the ground
and breathed into his nostrils the breath of life,
and the man became a living creature.*

GENESIS 2:7 ESV

Young parents anxiously await the birth of their child. This coming miracle, a result of their love for one another, will soon make its appearance and all the wondering about who the child will resemble most will be answered. As the mother labors to bring the baby forth, she listens for that first cry, watches for the first breath, and rejoices when it happens. A new life has begun.

The Bible says we are dust. It is strange to comprehend that God picked up a part of the earth and made man. Even more difficult to fathom is the intricacy within each one of us and how brilliantly he created us from particles of dirt. Reading this account in Scripture, we marvel at God's incomparable power and tremble in humility at his greatness. As we study further, we learn that the face of God comes close enough to give us the air we need to survive. The very breath of God fills our lungs, intimate and mighty, placing us on a journey to know him and love him.

Will you marvel today that you are an amazing work of art by God?

Welcomed

This is not the time to pull away and neglect meeting
together, as some have formed the habit of doing.
In fact, we should come together even more frequently,
eager to encourage and urge each other onward
as we anticipate that day dawning.

HEBREWS 10:25 TPT

We have all had lonely times in life. Perhaps our closest friend moved to a different state. Maybe we were so busy that we allowed ourselves to be consumed with the tasks at hand, ignoring our social life. Dire circumstances can even keep us trapped at home or unable to gather with loved ones. Whatever the cause, lack of human interaction can lead to both physical and mental distress.

God knew from the time he created Adam that it was not good for any of us to be alone. He made us for relationship with him and with each other. As the body of Christ, we are called to love one another and engage in communal worship. We are to look to the needs of others before our own. We can't do that if we are not involved in each other's lives. If we neglect to congregate, we can get out of practice and make excuses for not attending services. We need each other for encouragement, prayer, and support through this life.

Is attending church a constant in your life?

Witness

Faith comes by hearing,
and hearing by the word of God.

ROMANS 10:17 NKJV

You learn that a store is closing, and they are giving away all their remaining goods for free. Do you share the news? Or do you keep it to yourself so that you have a better chance of getting the best stuff? You hear on the news that a major storm is coming. Everyone should stay home, but you don't share the news with a family member, and they get stuck in the onslaught. What if someone discovered the cure for cancer and didn't share it with anyone? Unthinkable!

All these situations withhold a benefit or lifesaving information from others. When we do not share Jesus and ignore the great commission, we put people at risk of never hearing about salvation. They have no chance of coming to faith in Christ if they don't know the gospel. None of us want to see anyone separated from God for eternity, so why do we guard our knowledge of God's gift? We must pray for boldness and to love humanity with the heart of Jesus. He wants all to come to salvation.

Do you shrink back from sharing the good news? Who needs to hear the gospel today?

Affirmed

Today the LORD has proclaimed to you to be His special people, just as He promised you, that you should keep all His commandments.

DEUTERONOMY 26:18 NKJV

You studied diligently, and now it's graduation. Your family and friends are there to watch as you are awarded a special title for your career choice. After this, you are expected to put everything you learned into practice. What you do will trickle down to others, and as someone appointed to perform in your line of work, it is expected that you will faithfully follow through on the knowledge you have obtained.

To be called God's special people, his treasured possession, is the greatest description that could be given to us. With Jesus as our Savior, the Lord has promised that we are his precious children. As his spiritual offspring, we are to study his Word so that we can incorporate it into any situation at a moment's notice. It comforts us, gives us courage, and can keep us from choosing to sin. Scripture is God-breathed and living. When we commit to knowing it, we experience its life-giving ability. God asks us to follow his commands because he knows it is for our best and leads us to salvation.

Is memorizing Scripture a regular practice in your life?

Astute

With the one who is pure You show Yourself pure.
But with the perverted You show Yourself astute.

2 SAMUEL 22:27 NASB

No one likes being deceived. We want people to follow through
on what they say and be trustworthy and honest. There are true
stories of people embezzling funds from their employers or
taking off with a client's finances. Some of them escape the law
and now recline on a beach somewhere outside of jurisdiction.
When we believe in someone deceitful, we pay the price.

When God warns us in his Word, it is because he wants us
to take it to heart. His advice is meant to protect us. He wants
us to be wise, discerning, and able to recognize the type of
person we are dealing with. We are to act in the same manner
with those who are honorable. If someone is plotting evil, we
should be able to recognize it and be shrewd. If a believer is up
to no good, we should confront them with Scripture. If they
don't listen, we are to separate from that person. We should
remember to pray that God draws them to himself, so that they
will confess and receive forgiveness.

Have you been gullible lately, ignoring the wisdom of the Word?

Conducted

Even a child makes himself known by his acts,
by whether his conduct is pure and upright.

PROVERBS 20:11 ESV

Have you ever felt like you were being watched? It can be unsettling. Are you imagining things? You brush it off, but as you walk down the street, you realize you just can't shake the feeling. You start to get concerned. You hold your purse closer as you move toward a crowd for protection, and when you look back, you are relieved to see your pursuer turning down another street.

The world is watching us Christians. In this internet age, the scrutiny can feel more invasive than ever. This sounds daunting at first, but it is actually a positive thing. We have the chance to let our light shine in a dark world that is hungry for truth. As we walk with the Lord and let others see who Jesus is in us, they will find the answer they are looking for. We have a responsibility to represent Christ in a way that draws people to his saving grace. Let them see the truth in you!

When you leave home, are you doing it as an ambassador for Christ?

Conformable

Do not be conformed to this world, but be transformed
by the renewing of your mind, that you may prove what
is that good and acceptable and perfect will of God.
ROMANS 12:2 NKJV

Her parents told her to be careful as she left to hang out with a group for the evening. "Don't let anyone talk you into doing anything you know you shouldn't," her father advised. She promised she would not get talked into anything. When the group decided to take a risk and go somewhere off-limits, in the dark, she went but was frightened. The activity came to an end when she was the one hurt and taken to the hospital.

This world beckons us to follow its often-dangerous lead. When we succumb, we can find ourselves on the road to destruction. God's ways are opposite of the way of human knowledge. He wants us to ignore the trappings of this life and transform us, giving us the mind of Christ. Then we will be able to discern what is righteous and what is misguided. We have the power of the Holy Spirit to help us make choices that honor God and are for our good. We are not of this world, and we must not live like we are.

Who do you follow more: the world or Jesus?

Priority

> *"Seek the Kingdom of God above all else, and live righteously, and he will give you everything you need."*
>
> MATTHEW 6:33 NLT

If we kept a record of our daily activities, it would be a great way to see what we consider most important in our lives. It would reveal if we were a workaholic, self-centered, or only dedicated to our own entertainment. What we give our time to is a great indicator of where our hearts are and whether or not they are wrongfully divided.

We often run ragged trying to keep up, working to supply what we want and need, and it is so futile. God is more than able to give us all that we require and desire in his perfect wisdom and perfect provision. If we follow his commands, love him with all our hearts, souls, and minds, and live to serve him, we will never lack anything that he wants us to have. Jesus told us not to worry about what we will eat or what we will wear, for our heavenly Father will be our supplier.

Do you trust God to provide for you?

Enough

> *There is salvation in no one else! God has given no other name under heaven by which we must be saved.*
>
> ACTS 4:12 NLT

Have you ever known a die-hard perfectionist? No matter what the object of their dedication is, nothing is good enough. They rarely accept help because they believe only they are capable. We look and marvel, thinking that this person has achieved greatness in the task, but there is no convincing them. They try to improve on what is already masterful. Frustrated, they continue to revisit the drawing board.

Many believe that there are several ways to heaven, but we know the truth. The Word tells us that there is no other entrance besides Jesus. There are many false religions that tell you otherwise and many false prophets that seek to corrupt our faith. Only by accepting the sacrifice made for us in Christ's broken body and spilled blood will we be saved. No amount of works or service will add to God's free gift; it was finished on the cross. Aren't you thankful that our heavenly Father didn't leave it up to us? He sent his Son in our place.

Are you working for your salvation or trusting Jesus?

Firm

Stay true to the Lord. I love you and long to see you,
dear friends, for you are my joy and the crown
I receive for my work.

PHILIPPIANS 4:1 NLT

The mother faced down her opposer, determined to win the battle. She had said no when he voiced his viewpoint on the subject. She knew her reasons were justified, but her rival wouldn't budge. He had dug in his heels and refused to see things her way. Out of intense love for her toddler and for her own sanity, she stood her ground. She scooped him up, carrying the boy off for the nap he refused but definitely needed.

Did you know you are the apple of God's eye? His love for us is extravagant, and as our loving Father, he always works for good on our behalf. He sees our today and our tomorrow, and he alone can understand what we need before we even ask. He knows what he has called us to do for his kingdom, and he equips us to achieve it. He leads us to become more like his Son, transforming us into his likeness. He tells us to trust his ways and stand securely in our faith. When trials come, he will fight our battles for us as he leads us into victory for his glory.

Are you unwavering, secure in your faith? Where do you need to ask for strength?

Integrity

People with integrity walk safely,
but those who follow crooked paths will be exposed.
PROVERBS 10:9 NLT

Hidden misdeeds often come to the surface eventually, especially if it affects someone else. A confession of guilt can result from regret that eats away at the individual because they just couldn't live with themselves. When a wrongful action is revealed, it is a lesson for those who hear of the matter to always be truthful to live a life of peace and safety, free of discord.

God is so good to tell us how to conduct our lives through his Word. When we hide our sin, it is harmful to us—unhealthy, even—and the consequences that come from uncovered sin can cause great harm to those we love. If we understand how important truth is to our protection and to the testimony of Christ that we carry, we will desire and pray for the wisdom and discernment to live a life that could be clean if seen under a microscope. We can't do this on our own, but if we surrender and give Jesus lordship over our lives, he will help us to walk with him as we are transformed by his purity.

If you are hiding an unknown sin, will you confess it today?

November

✝

*That's why I take pleasure in my weaknesses, and
in the insults, hardships, persecutions,
and troubles that I suffer for Christ.
For when I am weak, then I am strong.*

2 Corinthians 12:10 NLT

Joy

The LORD is my strength and shield.
I trust him with all my heart.
He helps me, and my heart is filled with joy.
I burst out in songs of thanksgiving.

PSALM 28:7 NLT

Isn't it a relief when someone cares enough about you to protect you? Before seat belts were a law, many a mother would instinctively guard her young child with her arm while slamming on the brakes. You may have witnessed a young man or woman notice an elderly person struggle carrying their grocery bags. They step in to help so that the elder doesn't hurt themselves with the weight. Both instances guard someone in need against danger.

When you consider that you have a protector, who provides you with strength and covers you with a shield every hour of every day, it should evoke absolute faith in him. Our God keeps us in his care and gives us his gracious provision in all situations. Nothing escapes him; he sees anything that is a concern before it happens. He steps in with his might as our conqueror. This gives assured joy and absolute confidence that nothing can harm us. In his perfect will, God always deliver us until he returns to take us home. What a joyful day that will be!

Is anything stopping you from experiencing joy today? What dangers can you turn over to your protector?

Moral

Do not be deceived:
Evil company corrupts good habits.
1 Corinthians 15:33 NKJV

There was a popular game for church youth groups that disguised a vital life lesson. Two teens would be chosen and brought to the front of the room. A single chair was positioned before them. One teen would stand on the chair while the other stayed on the floor. The teens needed to find out which was easier: for the one on the chair to pull up the person on the ground, or for the one below to pull the other down. As multiple teams tried it, the result was always the same. It was much easier to pull the teenager on the chair down.

This game is a vivid example of how one can be influenced by the bad behavior of another and coerced to follow suite. When we are in relationship with someone whose morals are drastically lacking, we can pick up their habits. We are saved from sin by grace but will always be tempted while on this earth. It is crucially important to be discerning about who we spend time with. Be wise. Don't associate closely with someone of ill repute.

Do you consider the character of those you allow close to you?

Pardoned

*"Whenever you stand praying, forgive, if you have
anything against anyone, so that your Father also who is
in heaven may forgive you your trespasses."*

MARK 11:25 ESV

It hurts when we are wronged, especially if it is done knowingly
by another. It feels almost impossible to forget and even harder
to forgive. You want that person to own up to what they did, to
come to you in humility and confess. Then, you might find some
peace. But what if they never do? What do you do with that?

Maybe you said something innocently that harmed another.
When they come to you, will you defend yourself? Or will
you, in humility, realize that whether or not you meant to, you
caused that person pain? Will you be quick to ask for pardon?
It is a sobering thing to understand that if we don't forgive, God
won't forgive us. We have been absolved of so much through
the sacrifice of Jesus. How could we withhold forgiveness from
one another? There is no way to repay the debt Jesus paid
for us, but we show him our gratitude when we forgive as he
forgave us. It may be excruciatingly difficult to forgive and
forget, but through the power of the Holy Spirit, we can prevail.

*Do you need to seek forgiveness from someone? Is there someone
you haven't forgiven?*

Prepared

> *"There are many rooms in my Father's house;*
> *I would not tell you this if it were not true.*
> *I am going there to prepare a place for you."*
>
> JOHN 14:2 NCV

Thanksgiving is a holiday that takes massive preparation. From the recipe planning to the grocery list, there is a lot of work before the difficult task of cooking the meal. If you are hosting a large group, you worry if there will be enough. It can take weeks just to get ready for all the work you will be doing on one day. Then Christmas comes right on its heels! We are all too aware of how time-absorbing constructing and executing holidays can be.

Can you even begin to imagine the kind of planning that went into our heavenly home? Jesus told us in Scripture that he was leaving to make ready our home in heaven. When you read the exquisite details in Revelation, the streets of gold and jeweled gates, doesn't it thrill you? He will wipe the tears from our eyes, and we will experience a new body incapable of illness. The best part, though, is that we will live with him forever. He guarantees there are more than enough rooms. Go ahead and shout, "Come, Lord Jesus, come!"

As you visualize your heavenly home, will you praise God for his provision?

Relief

God is our refuge and strength,
A very ready help in trouble.
PSALM 46:1 NASB

Lois Lane sure had it good. If she ran into trouble or needed assistance with a simple task, Superman was there in a heartbeat. His extraordinary strength could keep a city bus from falling on her. If a bad guy approached her, he would swoop in and pummel the dude. He protected her from impending doom, always ready to pick her up and fly her to safety. Still, it is only a story.

As amazing as that story sounds, we have it much better because our defender is real. The one true God is our source of strength and our respite, and he has unequaled power. He hides us in the shadow of his wings. He fights our battles for us. He waits for us to come and seek him, but he moves on our behalf even if we miss our time with him. He is faithful even when we are not. When you are a child of God, you have a guarantee. He will never leave you or forsake you. He will be with you in times of trouble. He will guide you and deliver you. What blessed promises!

When trouble hits, do you go directly to God?

Revered

Those who feared the LORD talked with each other, and the LORD listened and heard. A scroll of remembrance was written in his presence concerning those who feared the LORD and honored his name.

MALACHI 3:16 NIV

The king decided to disguise himself and walk among his subjects, listening for what they might say about him. As he exited the castle, he wondered, would he be pleased? Was he considered a good king? Did the people respect him and know he had their best interests at heart, or did they believe he was only concerned about wealth and fame? As he moved indiscreetly, he heard only kind words for his leadership. His heart swelled, moving him to create a decree that would favor them.

Many people disregard the kindness of God, ignoring his gift of salvation. They use his name but only as a swear word. This breaks his heart, but when his children show reverence for him and offer prayers of thanksgiving and songs of praise, he is immensely pleased. God remembers those who acknowledge him for the loving, just God that he is. When we receive Christ, he writes our name in the book of life, a guarantee that we belong to him and will be accepted into his kingdom because of the sacrifice of Jesus. We are his, and he is ours.

How often do you speak words of God's praise to others?

Sensible

I remind you to fan into flame the gift of God.
For God gave us a spirit not of fear
but of power and love and self-control.
2 TIMOTHY 1:6-7 ESV

Events in life can cause rational or irrational fear. When we are driving and the person behind us is speeding or riding our back bumper, that concern is rational. If we are afraid to leave the house because of what might be out there, that is irrational. If a child thinks there is a monster under their bed, we check to assure them, even though we know there is no such thing. We all know, though, that terror can erupt into a mental monster, and we must conquer it.

We have no reason for dismay. God has already taken care of every issue. He is in control and has equipped us with all we need to shut anxiety down at the onset. We have been given power, love, and self-control in place of fear. There is nothing to dread for his power to overcome is in us. Don't give in to the feeble tactics of the enemy of your soul. When your adversary makes fear rear its ugly head in your direction, breathe, quote today's verse, believe it, and watch your dread dissipate.

How do you quiet your fear?

Sheltered

Those who live in the shelter of the Most High
will find rest in the shadow of the Almighty.
PSALM 91:1 NLT

Your long-awaited vacation has arrived. All your tropical clothes are packed, and you have plenty of sunscreen and a couple of good books. You have worked hard and waited eagerly for the day you would hop on a plane, and now that day is here. After checking into your hotel, you slip into your beachwear and head down to the sand, where a lovely cabana is waiting for you. You let out a sigh of relief, knowing you will now get some much-needed relaxation.

We all face trials and burdens in this life. When we endure these times, we are invited by our Creator to dwell under his wings. He wants to pull us close and comfort us. Jesus offers to share his yoke with us, and we know without a doubt that he will be pulling the weight. He invites us to come to him if we are weary. He will give us rest from our concerns. He has all the answers and can solve any problem. We just need to trust, be still, and stay close to the Deliverer.

What do you need to find rest from?

Tender

*Encourage one another daily, as long as it is called
"Today," so that none of you may be hardened
by sin's deceitfulness.*

HEBREWS 3:13 NIV

When none of her friends would acknowledge her
accomplishments, the woman wondered why. Were they
jealous, or was she not good enough? Was it her or her
abilities? Maybe she should try again, but right now, she just
wanted to cry. After she cried, she felt embarrassed. Next, her
anger boiled. How could they be so mean! She began plotting
her revenge. She would teach them to ignore her and her talent.

Do you think that really happens to people? Maybe not
that exact scenario, but there are many times when people
withhold their approval out of envy or apathy. God wants us
to encourage each other, spur one another on to good works,
and be champions for each other. We are the body of Christ,
and when someone uses their talents for good, we should
inspire that person. Without kind words of motivation and
acknowledgement, they could give up or get so discouraged that
it leads to sin. Let's be sincere in lifting each other up.

*When was the last time you spoke words of encouragement to
someone?*

Unselfish

Whoever is generous to the poor lends to the LORD,
and he will repay him for his deed.
PROVERBS 19:17 ESV

The friends walked into the restaurant, eager to converse and share a meal. Once seated at their table, the air was filled will stories and laughter. They reviewed the menu, and in their exuberance, they ordered a bit more than they needed or could finish. When the food arrived, they continued to chat as they ate, filling their stomachs to excess. Exiting with their takeout bags, they noticed a poor homeless man sitting by the door. Two of them ignored him, continuing to walk on their way with their leftovers. One stopped and handed him his bag and a twenty. "God bless you," he said as he left.

According to Scripture, the man who took pity and shared his food was sharing it with God. If the Lord cares about the sparrows, he desires that the needs of all people are met, especially when they are in need. It's his heart in us that moves us to be generous. Let's not be hoarders. Let's be the hands and feet of Jesus, providing out of our abundance to be a blessing to others.

Do you have items you could share with the poor? Could you volunteer your time with a worthy charity?

Valiant

"I, the LORD your God, hold your right hand;
it is I who say to you, 'Fear not,
I am the one who helps you.'"

ISAIAH 41:13 NIV

A young child ventured out into the front yard to play. Her mom said not to go near the street and stay only on the grass. Mom watched closely from inside the house, giving the girl a bit of independence but making sure she was alright. The ball bounced into the street. The child edged that way but stopped. Her mom ran out and asked, "Do you want to get your ball?" "I want to, but I need help," the girl replied. "Hold my hand; I'll walk with you," said her mother.

Whenever we have challenges in life that make us uneasy, God promises that if we ask him, he will assist us. Fear doesn't need to be a part of the equation, for our Lord is more than able. He promises to take us by the hand and lead us through any situation. There is nowhere we can go that he hasn't gone before us. He is our Father, and he has told us that he is for us and not against us. He has always been with us and always will be. He is faithful.

How does it make you feel, knowing God is holding your right hand?

Wanted

*"God so loved the world that He gave His only begotten
Son, that whoever believes in Him should not perish
but have everlasting life."*

JOHN 3:16 NKJV

Have you ever read O. Henry's story called "The Gift of the
Magi?" It's a short, beautiful story about a young, poor married
couple and their lack of funds to buy Christmas presents for
each other. In a nutshell, the wife cuts and sells her hair to buy
a chain for her husband's watch. The husband sells his watch
to buy a beautiful comb for her long hair. When they give each
other the gifts, they understand fully their depth of love for one
another by what they were willing to part with.

God gave everything to gain us. To think that God would
sacrifice his only Son to save us from our sin is staggering. We
are sinners who turned our backs on the Lord, yet he went to
extraordinary lengths so that we could be forgiven and become
his children. Even as he watched his precious Son being
tortured, he didn't change his mind. He didn't stop the horror
because he knew the glory it would bring. Jesus defeated the
grave; the veil was torn, and we received access to the Father.
There is no greater love.

If you have not received salvation, will you today?

Regarded

*See what kind of love the Father has given to us,
that we should be called children of God; and so we are.
The reason why the world does not know us
is that it did not know him.*

1 JOHN 3:1 ESV

A young diplomat made his way to the mansion for a special event that would honor his father, a well-known ambassador. It was an invitation-only affair that was protected by heavy security. No one without credentials would be allowed in, and no excuses accepted. When the son arrived, he reached in his pocket for his papers to verify who he was. Unfortunately, he had grabbed the wrong jacket, and the proof of his identity was in his other coat. He missed the ceremony because no one knew who he was.

As Christians, we are aliens in this world. We just don't belong. That should illicit songs of praise to flow from our lips, for we are sons and daughters of God. We belong to a much better kingdom as citizens of heaven. The world doesn't understand us because they do not accept the truth of God's Word and the salvation of his Son. Thankfully, we know the outcome at the end of this world, and our victory is sure. We must pray for the lost, that their eyes will be opened, and they will be saved.

Are you concerned about the salvation of others?

Sure

"This is the confidence we have in approaching God:
that if we ask anything according to his will,
he hears us."

JOHN 5:14 NIV

Imagine preparing long and hard to give a presentation before a large group who had the authority to help you or squash your idea. You did your research, crafted a few witty sayings, and felt that you would receive a warm welcome. They day of your speech comes, and you walk confidently into the room. Think of your surprise when, halfway through, you start to see yawns and a few people nodding off. Discouraged, you realize that your proposal has fallen on deaf ears.

When we take our concerns before the throne of grace, we are assured that God will be faithful to hear us. We need not raise our voice to make sure he is within earshot, for he is always eagerly waiting to hear from his child. If our petition is within his good and perfect will, we can believe in faith that he will grant us the very thing we are asking for. Come with faith, the right motive, and complete surrender to his will, and you can be sure that you will receive what you have asked of him.

Do you check your heart motives before you pray?

Alert

"I say to everyone—
be awake at all times."
MARK 13:37 TPT

We live in interesting times. Every day, there is some new crisis on the horizon, and the whole world is on edge. We are hit with information from every direction, whether it is online, in print, or on television. With our sophisticated technology, we have progressed to a place where we can see domestic and international developments in real time. Our society knows far more these days than we did twenty or thirty years ago.

When considering world events, we Christians might be led to believe that we are getting closer and closer to end times. Jesus made it clear that only the Father knows the day of his return, not even the Son. But we are told to be aware, to be watchful and discern the times. Jesus will return in the twinkling of an eye. We need to live with urgency, sharing the gospel and looking for his coming.

Have you studied what the Bible says about the coming end times?
Are you living in preparation?

Confident

I can do all things through him who strengthens me.
PHILIPPIANS 4:13 ESV

A large percentage of our population is hooked on physical exercise. There are programs and gyms galore that will help you reach your goal. Home equipment is manufactured with screens that can turn your stationary bike into a destination overseas. The danger is that working out can become a personal idol. It can become a never-ending cycle of attempting to reach the height of an impossible goal, no matter how long or hard you try.

As humans, we have limitations. Many of us can accomplish things that others can't and vice versa. As Christians, we have a supernatural ability to attain any objective because the power of Christ enables us. We must place our confidence in Jesus for the task ahead, for without him we can do nothing. Even with faith like a mustard seed, the miraculous can come to pass. It is Jesus who supplies us with his power and strength. Through him, all things are possible.

When you need strength for a looming task, do you attempt it on your own or go directly to the Savior?

Earnest

Without faith it is impossible to please God, because anyone who comes to him must believe that he exists and that he rewards those who earnestly seek him.

HEBREWS 11:6 NIV

If you went to summer camp as a kid or teenager, you probably have fond memories of the activities. From campfires to meals in the cafeteria, you made new friendships and strengthened old ones. There may have been a team-building time that included a trust fall. That is when you let go of your body and fall backwards, believing that the person behind you will catch you and not allow you to end up in the dirt.

Hebrews tells us that without faith, we cannot please God. If we are going to make a request of him, we need to believe that he will answer us. We must acknowledge his character, that he is an all-powerful God that keeps his word. If we doubt what the Word tells us, we are like a wave of the sea, thrown here and there by the wind, and we should not expect anything from the Lord. And when we receive our answer, we must remember that even if it differs from what we wanted, our wise and loving heavenly Father has answered in a way that is best for us.

Are your prayers doubtful or trusting?

Covered

Keep me as the apple of your eye;
hide me in the shadow of your wings.
PSALM 17:8 ESV

The farmer believed he had a home with a sturdy roof, but as it was in an area that had seasonal tornadoes, he made sure to include a basement when the house was constructed. He had a wife and children that he dearly loved. He would leave nothing to chance. If a horrible storm did occur, his family could take shelter and emerge from the onslaught unscathed. This made his loved ones feel cared for and safe, and it gave the farmer peace of mind.

We have a God whose care for us is nothing short of extravagant and all-encompassing. Not only does he call us his personal treasure, but he also gave the one he valued the most, his precious Son, as a sacrifice for our sin. He sings over us and protects us in the shadow of his wings. He knows the number of hairs on our heads. Our Father provides for us more intricately than for the lilies of the field. His is the greatest love of all, and it is promised to those who love him for all of eternity.

Do you have trouble believing the immense love God has for you?

Esteemed

The LORD said to Samuel, "Don't look at how handsome Eliab is or how tall he is, because I have not chosen him. God does not see the same way people see. People look at the outside of a person, but the LORD looks at the heart."

1 SAMUEL 16: 7 NLT

Our culture puts most of a person's importance on the way they look. Magazines yearly rank the world's 100 most beautiful women. Beauty is in the eye of the beholder, but we tend to take to heart that those listed are the gold standard. If you don't have the lauded features, figure, hair, or skin, you must do all you can to get as close as you can. This can lead to insecurity and a never-ending pursuit to find any and all ways to compare to these celebrities.

Even Samuel, when looking for the man of God's choosing, had it wrong. He assumed that the most handsome would be first choice. Thankfully, the Lord stepped in and made his choice. God does not judge by the world's shallow beauty standards. He considers most crucial the motive and condition of our hearts. Aren't you thankful that we don't have to measure up to this society's false idea of glamor? We have a heavenly father who has made it clear what he considers beautiful.

Do you spend more time on your outward or inward appearance?

Fortitude

> *"If the world hates you, know that it has hated me before it hated you. If you were of the world, the world would love you as its own; but because you are not of the world, but I chose you out of the world, therefore the world hates you."*
>
> JOHN 15:18-19 ESV

The debate team was entering the competition arena. They were ready to meet their rivals and present their argument confidently. Their class had carefully studied tactics to attack sharply differing views from a stance of emotional indifference. However, as the topic grew heated, each student took words spoken about their subject to heart, and it became obvious that the intent to remain unmoved had been unsuccessful. Bad feelings were evident in the attitudes of the participants.

Jesus warned us that the world would not understand our belief or commitment to him. Some would see us as lunatics or as snobs, assuming we think ourselves higher than others. Opposers ridicule and try to silence believers. In some areas of the world, Christians are persecuted, tortured by evil organizations who insist they recant their faith or endure more torment. This is heartbreaking but not surprising, for Jesus said the world would hate us. When they do, we must respond in love. We must help them see Jesus, regardless of any personal risk.

As tensions in the world heighten, are you prepared to stand firm for your faith?

Gentle

A soft answer turns away wrath,
But a harsh word stirs up anger.
PROVERBS 15:1 NKJV

The first few months of the relationship were magical. Both parties were on their best behavior, wanting to please the other person as much as possible. They always insisted the other person choose first. For a time, they agreed with one another even when they really didn't, but eventually, that started to bother them. Instead of discussing it, they let their internal anger increase until it broke forth. Hurtful things were said that couldn't be taken back.

God knew we would need self-control over our words. In James, he gives us the vivid description of the tongue as a raging fire from hell, one that is full of deadly poison. Misspoken words have destroyed friendships, dissolved business partnerships, and started wars. Pain caused by a careless conversation can damage and remain with someone for years to come. Scripture tells us to be kind and gentle, to speak encouraging words to one another. When we converse, it is to be done in love and purity, which is pleasing to our Savior and builds others up in the faith.

Have you had success lately in controlling your tongue?

Gratitude

Rejoice always, pray without ceasing,
give thanks in all circumstances;
for this is the will of God in Christ Jesus for you.
1 THESSALONIANS 5:16-18 ESV

There is a big difference in the reaction of someone who opens a present they wanted versus receiving something they will never use. They may smile and be polite, but if the person is honest and is only hiding their feelings to spare another's, it may still be obvious they are less than pleased. If a child is the recipient, it is far more apparent that they are unhappy. They wanted that new superhero toy, not more pajamas!

There is no guarantee that life will always be sunny. In fact, Jesus said we would have trouble in this world. When things go awry, the Word instructs us to react with gratitude, knowing that our God sees and is in control of everything. We should pray our needs and questions, not stopping until we have direction from the Lord. It is God's perfect will that we live in ways that emulate Jesus and show the joy of belonging to him. We are representatives of Christ, and as we live a prayerful, exuberant existence, we share the living message of him with the world.

What will you rejoice about today?

Intuitive

All Scripture is breathed out by God and profitable for teaching, for reproof, for correction, and for training in righteousness, that the man of God may be complete, equipped for every good work.

2 TIMOTHY 3:16-17 ESV

When we have an instructor who is gifted and thorough, and we are paying attention, we have a great opportunity for growth. A well-taught course has several goals in mind, from adding to our intellect on the topic to training us to someday utilize it. If we have a misunderstanding of the concept and blurt it out, certain that we know more than the learned teacher, we leave ourselves open to disapproval and possibly an embarrassing reprimand.

The Word of God is the only book in existence that is alive. He used men chosen by his will to speak his truth. He left us a guidebook, created in love, to give us commands to live by. Scripture teaches, trains, convicts us of sin, and presents the gospel of Jesus Christ to forgive us and bring us to salvation. It tells us how to conduct ourselves and tells of the comforter, the Holy Spirit, who is with us until we are called home. If we commit to study and retain God's Word, we will walk in a manner that honors him, ready to give an answer for our faith.

When is the last time you memorized a verse?

Thankful

*Give thanks for everything to God the Father
in the name of our Lord Jesus Christ.*

EPHESIANS 5:20 NLT

Certain titles can get people into places that others can't.
Celebrities can likely walk into any exclusive venue and be
admitted immediately, even without a ticket. Doctors have
been known to get better tables at a restaurant just because of
the professional initials in front of their name. Perhaps you or
someone you know is acquainted with a person whose moniker
allows you into events with special treatment. In this case, you
are no doubt grateful you were permitted to use their name.

God gives us blessings that most of us take for granted or
wrongfully believe we deserve. We can forget from day to day
that these things are granted only by our Lord. Every morning
we breathe is because God ordains it. The Word says to be
thankful for everything and to daily remember the magnificent
things God's grace has bestowed upon us. When we praise
God for all he has done for us, we're to do it in the name that is
above all names: that of our precious Savior, Jesus Christ.

What are you most thankful for today?

Necessary

*Most important of all, continue to show deep love
for each other, for love covers a multitude of sins.*

1 PETER 4:8 NLT

Have you ever heard that love is a choice? Or that if you actively do things to show your love for someone, the feelings will follow? We can get aggravated over the pettiest things and remove ourselves and our affection from someone. We have been offended and we want the person who did it to know it. What if we showed compassion instead? We might not know what caused them to react that way. Maybe that person is suffering. We can choose to take the high road and forgive, even if they don't ask for it.

We are to love abundantly and unconditionally, most importantly for others' benefit and oftentimes the good of the body of Christ. Nothing causes dissension in the church like division over wrongs done, gossip and rumors, and differences of opinions that neither side will budge on. This is why God tells us to live at peace, bear one another's burdens, and forgive as Christ forgave us. If we choose to love others sacrificially and sincerely, we can fulfill God's desire to avoid sin.

Are you willing to forgive and forget for the good of others?

Perceptive

Do not love the world or anything in the world. If anyone loves the world, love for the Father is not in them.

1 JOHN 2:15 NIV

There is a way to watch TV that is called "bingeing." Streaming channels present multiple seasons of series at all once, enabling us to watch hour upon hour of one show in a sitting. Addicted to viewing television in this fashion, we brag about the fact that we finished a whole season in one night. We're obsessed, giving precious hours of life to something that really doesn't offer much benefit to our lives.

When we allow entertainment or objects to become our primary focus, we are allowing ourselves to get entrapped with things the world values. If we kept a schedule of how much time we spend on things that have no heavenly value, we would most likely shudder at the inequality. Doesn't this indicate what we consider important in our lives? Maybe this is why God reminds us not to love the world or what it values. If we are committed to the Father with love and devotion, we will want to spend more time in his presence rather than with things that will one day pass away.

If you tracked your time, what do you think it would reveal to you?

Willpower

We all experience times of testing, which is normal for every human being. But God will be faithful to you. He will screen and filter the severity, nature, and timing of every test or trial you face so that you can bear it. And each test is an opportunity to trust him more, for along with every trial God has provided for you a way of escape that will bring you out of it victoriously.

1 CORINTHIANS 10:13 TPT

We all know about resolutions. Most of us have made them. Even if we didn't prevail the last time we committed, each year we are determined that this time we will succeed. We set little goals, providing rewards for ourselves as we arrive at each mile marker. We breeze along and then, out of nowhere, we are hit with the one thing that will tip the scales toward failure. We look away, close our eyes, distance ourselves, and wait to see if we will be able to resist or not.

Jesus told us we would have trials in life, and he warned us that we have an enemy who is an evil, lurking snake who will go to any lengths to trip us up. What our accuser forgets is that with Christ, we have all we need to be victorious when it comes to temptation. Call out, for God is on watch. He will never leave us to fend for ourselves, and he has given us the power of the Holy Spirit to combat and win against the devil's schemes.

Knowing Satan will attack, are you putting on the armor of God daily?

Victorious

In all these things we are more than conquerors through him who loved us.

ROMANS 8: 37 NIV

There is a father and son team that compete in athletic challenges together. They have biked, run, and even taken on the difficult Ironman competition. Their participation looks different from others, though, because the son is disabled by cerebral palsy. The father provides special equipment that his son can sit in while he pushes and provides the running legs that move them both. If swimming is involved, they have a special boat the son rides in while his dad swims and pushes it. Together, they have never quit a race, and what drives them is their intense love for one another.

When it comes to triumph in our lives, Scripture tells us that we far exceed what we could imagine as victors. It has nothing to do with us and everything to do with the one who sacrificially gave his life to save us by suffering in our place. Once we receive Jesus as our Savior, we receive the full benefit of his victory over the grave. We have been given every advantage, every gift, and his Holy Spirit's power, and it is all because he loves us so very much.

Do you live like you are an overcomer?

Truthful

> *"If you abide in My word,*
> *you are My disciples indeed.*
> *And you shall know the truth,*
> *and the truth shall make you free."*
>
> JOHN 8:31-32 NKJV

When the policeman flashed his lights in her direction, she froze. Pulling over, she started to sweat, even though she was uncertain of what she had done wrong. The officer approached her car and asked, "Do you know you were going fifty in a thirty-five?" She replied she that she didn't think there was a speed limit on the country road. "You should know and obey the law. I will have to give you a ticket," he scolded.

Jesus is the only way, truth, and life. To escape eternal death, we must come to Christ and confess our sin, receiving him as our Savior. As Christ's followers, we should want to study, memorize, and carry his Word in our hearts so that we can obey him. His Word instructs us in every area of life and leads us toward Christ's likeness. When we die to our flesh and live for Jesus, exhibiting the fruit of the Spirit, we are less likely to fall prey to temptation. His Word teaches that we are no longer slaves to sin. We are free.

Are you a studious disciple of God's Word or a casual one?

Successful

You will show me the way of life,
granting me the joy of your presence
and the pleasures of living with you forever.
PSALM 16:11 NLT

If you know a dedicated dog owner, you know the closeness of the relationship between animal and master. The very phrase "pet parent" has evolved due to so many adults treating their four-legged friends like their children. As human and canine play, you see the gleeful admiration in the wagging tail. When the ball is thrown, the puppy bounds after it, and the man calls for it to return for another round. When the pet obeys, it is rewarded for its success with a much-wanted treat and another throw of the ball.

We are not dogs, but in the same way, we are to delight in our master. When we are joyful over the love and attention of our heavenly Father, it gives him great satisfaction. We would do well to remember we were made specifically for his pleasure. As we show our admiration for our awesome God, he responds by giving us the deepest longing of our hearts. If we're walking with him, we know that our greatest desire will be fulfilled as the Father draws us closer into intimacy with him.

Do you aim to succeed in pleasing the Lord?

December

Search for the LORD and for his strength;
continually seek him.

1 CHRONICLES 16:11 NLT

Still

The LORD will fight for you,
and you have only to keep still.
EXODUS 14:14 NRSV

The neighborhood park buzzed with chatter as the youngsters surrounded and egged on the two in the circle to raise their fists. The younger boy cowered in the shadow of the older, larger boy. As shouts of "Chicken!" started to rise, the smaller one fought back tears. When the older child called him a sissy, he felt someone grab the back collar of his shirt. The onlookers gasped as they recognized the younger one's older, and much bigger, brother. He was bigger than any of the kids present. The little one stood tall, and no one bothered him again.

When we face unpleasant situations that offend or hurt us and we are the innocent party, we need to wait on God. He never wants us to take matters into our own hands without coming to him in prayer for guidance and wisdom. We must never seek vengeance or plot to repay evil for evil. As we listen for his voice, he will reveal if we are to act and what he would have us do. He wants us to stay dependent on him, and he will set things straight in his perfect way, timing, and will.

Do you let anger rule you, or God?

Resplendent

Splendid and majestic is His work,
And His righteousness endures forever.

PSALM 111:3 NASB

Incredible sights, like the massive Grand Canyon or the grandeur of towering mountain peaks, make it hard to deny that there is a vastly intelligent creator. When you stop to smell the fragrance of a budding rose or watch a colony of ants as they busily scurry, you cannot refute that this earth and its inhabitants are the result of the most creative mind in existence. At the first cry of a newborn babe, we bow to the brilliance and intricacy knitted together by the hands of the designer of life.

There is no doubt in the minds of believers that everything on this earth was made by God Almighty. It is hard for those of us who know him to understand how anyone would not recognize the glory of his handiwork. Not only did he form it all with precise perfection, but he did it out of love and according to his righteous and holy will. His work, whether that be us or his coming kingdom, will last for eternity. All that he made will praise his holy name.

Do you regard God's creation with praise and wonder?

Preferred

Do nothing from selfish ambition or conceit,
but in humility count others
more significant than yourselves.

PHILIPPIANS 2:3 ESV

The young executive noticed great talent in the intern and saw
a real advantage in enlisting her to work on his new project.
The intern hit it out of the park with her proposal, but when
it came time to take it to the CEO, the executive conveniently
left the trainee out. The head of the company loved the pitch
and praised the associate in front of the entire work force.
He noted that the intern's face fell at the announcement of
congratulations. Intuitively, he figured things out, and the
executive who took advantage of the intern was warned and put
on probation.

When we engage with others from a stance of humility, looking
out for their welfare, we are fulfilling God's desire for us.
There is no place for a Christian to act out of concern for only
their own benefit or advancement. If that is the condition of a
believer's heart, then that person must take inventory of their
surrender to Jesus. A sincere confession will bring meekness
and prepare a Christian to look to the needs of others, not
pursue their own honor above others.

Honestly, do others come first in your heart?

Courage

Wait for the LORD;
be strong, and let your heart take courage;
wait for the LORD!
PSALM 27:14 NRSV

Waiting to hear on a new job or a college acceptance letter can be hard. While you are in limbo, waiting for the response you hope will come, you can have a myriad of thoughts, from "I know I'll get this" to "it's never going to happen." You are on a roller coaster of emotions, and you try as hard as you can to subdue your concerns. Still, you wake up in the middle of the night and it's on your mind.

When life hands us moments where we languish as we wait for a decision that is in the hands of someone else, Scripture gives us a strategy. We are to depend on God, for the result is truthfully in his hands and his alone. He has a destiny for each life, and he'll bring it about in his timing. We are to hang in there, be brave, and believe our Lord is faithful and will fulfill his good and perfect plan for us. Our part is to love him with all our hearts, souls, and minds and to obey him. He will handle the rest.

Do you wait for God or rush ahead of him?

Charitable

You yourselves know that these hands of mine have supplied my own needs and the needs of my companions. In everything I did, I showed you that by this kind of hard work we must help the weak, remembering the words the Lord Jesus himself said: "It is more blessed to give than to receive."

ACTS 20:34-35 NIV

The family decided that they would have a different type of Christmas this year. They all agreed that instead of giving one another gifts, they would sponsor a needy family, one who would have nothing for the holidays unless generosity was shown to them. When they delivered the goodies on Christmas Eve, there was heartfelt thanks from the parents and their wide-eyed, smiling children. The true blessing was the glow felt in the hearts of the givers as they watched the joy of the recipients and how deeply they were touched.

It is so accurate that it is far better to give than it is to receive. When you make another's life better by sacrificing and sharing, it will fill you with immense delight. We have more than we could ever hope for in Christ. He wants us to treat others as he has treated us, giving our best to help those who need it. We are the hands and feet of Jesus when we look out for the cares of others.

What have you been given that you could share with others? Who needs more blessings?

Agreeable

The wisdom that comes from God is first of all pure,
then peaceful, gentle, and easy to please. This wisdom is
always ready to help those who are troubled and to do
good for others. It is always fair and honest.

JAMES 3:17 NCV

The man was plain old cantankerous. No matter what anyone said, he would disagree and insistently claim the opposite. He voiced his opinion even when no one asked what he thought. Most people avoided conversations with him because no matter what they said, he would be displeased and argumentative. Even his family members limited the time they spent with him and learned to drown him out in their minds as he raged on. They all chalked it up to a lack of prudence.

Believers in Christ are to walk in step with the Holy Spirit to develop the use of his fruit: love, joy, peace, patience, kindness, goodness, faithfulness, gentleness, and self-control. This helps us avoid temptations of the flesh. We will serve others and be ready to assist anyone experiencing hardship. We will be truthful, tranquil, and tender. We will not be difficult to deal with but enjoyable to be around. If we live a pure life, we will be wise, and we will carry the reputation of Jesus well.

Which fruit of the Spirit do you need to work on developing
the most?

Awe-Inspiring

When the crowd saw this, they were filled with awe; and they praised God, who had given such authority to man.
MATTHEW 9:7-8 NIV

If you have ever been to a professional magic show, you know they can perform feats that boggle the mind. Magicians can fool us into believing that their illusions are authentic. We are mystified as we watch, but we know it is only slight of hand. And while we are aware that all the *abracadabras* and wand waving are deception, at the end of the show, we cheer and applaud for being so enchantingly entertained.

Unlike a magic hoax, God's acts are undeniably real, supernatural, and full of incomparable power. When Jesus walked the earth, he did an abundance of miracles, so many that the Bible couldn't contain them all. When people gathered to see the wonders that Jesus wrought, they were astonished and gave glory and honor to God. They knew he was special. Some rightfully believed that he was the Messiah, for they had never seen anyone who spoke or moved with such authority. Since God is the same yesterday, today, and forever, we should keep our eyes open for his mighty wonders.

Do you believe that God still performs miracles?

Safety

In peace I will lie down and sleep,
for you alone, O LORD, will keep me safe.
PSALM 4:8 NLT

The young girl's mother checked under the bed one more time to prove there were no monsters, kissed her daughter, and turned out the light. Just as the woman climbed into her own bed and pulled up the covers, she heard the cry of the child, begging her mommy to come back. "You didn't check the closet!" the young one exclaimed. Wanting to assure the little one that she was safe, the mother carefully inspected the closet to assuage any fear. This time, she kissed her daughter and prayed with her before she left the room.

We have security systems, cameras on our front doors, or good old-fashioned padlocks to make us feel protected. We could add a steel door at every entry and they still wouldn't do what only our God can do. He is on constant watch, providing for our safety and supplying us with peace. He'll never leave us or forsake us, so there is no reason to fear and every reason to exist peacefully as his watchful eye guards us night and day.

When you go to bed at night, do you put your faith in God's presence?

Compassionate

"In everything, do to others what you would have them do to you, for this sums up the Law and the Prophets."
MATTHEW 7:12 NIV

You never want to get between two dogs fighting over the same meaty bone. There are always streams of tears when two toddlers grapple over the same beloved toy. Two teenaged girls who are besties and like the same boy can find themselves competing fiercely. And when two women each have a hold of one arm of a cashmere sweater that is on clearance, you had better get out of their way!

Even once we are saved by the grace of God, we still face temptations that lure us to believe we alone should get the gold. We have an innate desire to please ourselves and take what we believe we deserve. It dates back to Eve. She had a plethora of trees and fruit to pick from in the garden. She fixated on one and then brought Adam in to share the shame. If we want to follow Christ, we will treat others as we would like them to treat us. In fact, if we really want to be like Jesus, we will put the needs of others ahead of our own and humbly consider them first.

Would you sacrifice yourself for the good of another?

Support

> *The name of the LORD is a strong tower;*
> *the righteous runs into it and is safe.*
>
> PROVERBS 18:10 NASB

When the girls' soccer team started the game, the sun was shining, and the air was warm. As they progressed through the first period, the sky started to fill with clouds. At the beginning of half time, a few drops began to fall. At the start of the second period, the rain poured down, but they still played on, giggling at each other as they became covered with mud. When the first sign of lightning struck, however, it was no longer a laughing matter. They hightailed it back to the locker room.

Are there times in life when you tough it out, trying to resolve struggles on your own, only to find out you have made it worse? When we face predicaments beyond our ability to fix, we have a God who invites us to hurry to him so he can surround and protect us. We are never left or intended to handle the hardships of life on our own. We have a heavenly father who wants to gather us as a mother hen collects her chicks and comforts them. He is our great deliver.

Do you panic over crisis, or do you go to God?

Respect

Love one another with brotherly affection.
Outdo one another in showing honor.
ROMANS 12:10 ESV

The enlisted soldiers had trained well and were prepared to go overseas and serve their country. This was their first tour of duty; they understood the danger but had yet to experience it. They stood in the terminal, saying goodbye to their friends and loved ones. There were long hugs that were repeated, open and hidden tears. Families, friends, and soldiers wanted to be strong for each other.

Our freedom has come at a great cost to many others. Brave men and women put their lives at risk so that we can enjoy our lives at home. We must always show our gratitude, respect, and support for our honorable armed services and veterans. Like a soldier, Jesus sacrificed his life for the world. He showed the greatest love of all by atoning for our sins and saving us from eternal destruction. If we have the daily motive of outdoing one another in love and service, we will bring great honor to the cause of Christ.

What can you add to the way you love that will exemplify Jesus?

Triumphant

Thanks be to God, who in Christ always leads us in triumphal procession, and through us spreads the fragrance of the knowledge of him everywhere.

2 CORINTHIANS 2:14 ESV

Do you remember playing follow the leader as a child? A line of children would walk behind the youngster in front and imitate their actions as they trailed behind. It could be an imaginary hike through the jungle or an exhibition of silly arm-waving and high-stepping marches. It could include making animal sounds too. It was always adventurous and always fun.

Once we have come to Christ, he lives in us as our constant companion. Wherever we go, we take him with us. That can make us think twice if we are headed somewhere we would rather not have him see. Hopefully, that is not the case. One thing we can count on is that he will guide us in the direction that is best for us. He sees the future, and he is already there on our behalf, preparing the way. We are blessed and can bless others on this life journey with Jesus if we allow his love to flow through us. Then everywhere we go, we'll leave an impression of him that can lead others to his salvation.

How do you take God with you wherever you go?

Vulnerable

He said to me, "My grace is sufficient for you, for my power is made perfect in weakness." Therefore, I will boast all the more gladly about my weaknesses, so that Christ's power may rest on me. That is why, for Christ's sake, I delight in weaknesses, in insults, in hardships, in persecutions, in difficulties. For when I am weak, then I am strong.

2 CORINTHIANS 12: 9-10 ESV

An obstacle course was scheduled for the birthday party. The young girls met at the venue, giggling with anticipation. The tasks were manageable for most. Only one guest struggled as the group approached the final step. She was born with one leg shorter than the other, and the final jump was beyond her ability. Instead of just cheering her on, the group of girls lifted her into the air and helped her over the last bump. Because of their assistance, the goal was easily attained, and she felt loved in the process.

Most feel discouraged when they are incapable of doing something, but as believers, we can rejoice in our inability. When we strive alone to achieve something out of our reach, we set ourselves up for failure. If we accept our lack and surrender to Jesus, asking him to give us his power to overcome, then we move in his strength. Our hardship becomes victory because of our Savior's miraculous skill. Then we can testify that Christ delivered us and bring glory to his name.

How can you ask for the power of Jesus to help you?

Unwavering

Our hope for you is firmly grounded,
knowing that as you are partners in our sufferings,
so also you are in our comfort.

2 Corinthians 1:7 nasb

The three women really wanted a service project where they could work together for the good of another. They prayed about an opportunity, and God in his faithfulness answered. There was an older couple that desperately needed help with just about everything. Eventually, the needs of the elderly people got a bit overwhelming. Two of the women got tired of the constant requests and felt they had to bow out. The remaining woman decided to stick with it, and her relationship with the older couple deepened. She ended up getting far more out of the friendship than she felt she put in.

We can get weary of praying the same request for years. Waiting for someone we are discipling to really commit to giving Jesus control of their lives can get discouraging. Some days we just want to throw in the towel. If we believe Scripture, we will soldier on. God promises that if we persist, we'll see the evidence of our faith. It might be hard and exhausting, but if we're doing it to serve Christ, it will be worth it.

Do you tend to give up easily or stay the course for Christ?

Rest

God blessed the seventh day and made it holy,
because on it God rested from all his work
that he had done in creation.

GENESIS 2:3 ESV

The newlyweds bought a home that was a dilapidated fixer upper. They knew that it would take a lot of elbow grease and care to make the residence livable. And yet, they were excited. They dove in, doing almost all the work themselves. They spent weekdays, evenings, weekends, and months on end pouring themselves into the project. Almost a year later, it was time to move in. Once settled, they took a full day just to rest and enjoy the fruit of their labor.

God understands how important it is to take time off. He spent six days, according to his timetable, creating the heavens and the earth out of a formless void. He commissioned the sun to shine by day and the moon at night. Then came the sky, water, ground, vegetation, and all kinds of creatures. He created man and woman, breathing his own air into their lungs. Day seven, the Sabbath, was called his holy day of rest, not because he was weary, but so that he could sit back and commemorate all the miraculous good work he had done.

Are you a workaholic, or do you follow God's example of rest?

Received

Don't just listen to God's word.
You must do what it says.
Otherwise, you are only fooling yourselves.
JAMES 1:22 NLT

Did your parents ever use the phrase, "Do as I say, not as I do?" Words are important, but seeing an action played out before your eyes seems to stick better and replay in your memory. Both are equally critical. We need to watch what we say and how we behave. Imagine a toddler blurts out a bad word. When the dad asks where he learned it, the little one says, "From you, daddy." You can imagine how that father's heart sank.

When it comes to God's Word, we are to read, listen, and then follow through in obedience. Scripture is meant to inform us how to live in a Christ-worthy manner, and once we learn this, our action is required. If we ignore this truth, the Bible says that we are deceiving ourselves. The Word is alive, and it can leap off the page and embed in our hearts and minds. Make the effort to know Scripture so the Holy Spirit can work in us to produce fruit from the good works that God prepared in advance for us to do.

Do you just read the Word, or do you act on it?

Amazed

All the people were amazed and said,
"Perhaps this man is the Son of David!"
MATTHEW 12:23 NCV

The crowd gasped as the man they knew for so long to be blind and deaf stood before Christ. This man was not in this condition by purely medical reasons but was possessed by a demon. As the people watched, they were astonished as the man spoke and could see. Can you imagine what went through their minds? Did they really see the miracle they just witnessed? This man cast out a demon, a phenomenal feat. Maybe this was the Messiah they had been looking and hoping for.

We read about the supernatural healings of Jesus, but can you imagine what it would have been like to be present as they occurred? These people had physical, personal proof of what God could do. All they had to do was accept what they had witnessed in person and who Christ was and they would be saved. And yet we, who have not seen him, are amazed and believe based on the Word. We love him, see him with the eyes of our hearts, and we praise him with inexpressible joy. We serve a great and awesome God!

Are you a Thomas who still needs proof, or do you believe?

Approval

Am I now seeking human approval, or God's approval?
Or am I trying to please people?
If I were still pleasing people,
I would not be a servant of Christ.

GALATIANS 1:10 NRSV

Three women had been friends for years, and they prided themselves on how well they got along. One day, two of the ladies had a disagreement that went from a quiet discussion to a heated debate. The third lady stayed calm, but it was very clear to her who was in the right and who was in the wrong. She was in a quandary over what she should do. If she voiced her opinion, she would surely anger someone. Should she speak the truth regardless of the risk?

In a world where so many are opposed to the gospel, living as believers can place us in situations where people are judgmental and reject us for our beliefs. We need to know in advance what we will do in those situations. Many of our brethren in other parts of the world suffer greatly for their faith. Are we willing to face persecution? We need to decide where our loyalty is before the assault arises. Will we back down, or will we stand for Christ?

Where does your loyalty lie?

Righteous

I regard everything as loss because of the surpassing value of knowing Christ Jesus my Lord. For his sake I have suffered the loss of all things, and I regard them as rubbish, in order that I may gain Christ and be found in him, not having a righteousness of my own that comes from the law, but one that comes through faith in Christ, the righteousness from God based on faith.

PHILIPPIANS 3:8-9 NRSV

When a young woman was asked to add content to a work project in a dishonest way, she refused. She knew in her heart she could never compromise her morals for her employer but was concerned what that would mean. As she expected, her boss didn't understand why she was making such a big deal about it and became angry. If she would not do things his way, he would fire her. She shared that as a believer in Christ, she would rather lose her job than displease her Savior.

People have vast differences of opinions on the Christian lifestyle, and some lose friends and family members when they come to Jesus. Having no righteousness of our own, we cannot do anything to bring about our salvation. It is only through Jesus and his sacrifice that we are saved and made righteous in him. We choose Christ first and foremost, for he is our only hope.

If you had to give up absolutely everything to gain Christ, would you?

Sovereign

Our God is in heaven;
he does whatever pleases him.
PSALM 115:17 NIV

There are things in life we cannot control. Time marches on without anyone's approval. The sun rises and sets every day, thankfully, and we can count on its light to illuminate our way. Autumn leaves fall, winter cold chills our bones, spring flowers burst with color, and summers bring long-awaited vacations. Seasons change, and while we enjoy the variation that each part of the year provides, we have no say in it. It will continue with or without us.

The Lord God Almighty rules from his throne in heaven. He speaks and miracles happen. He's all-powerful, and he reigns sovereignly over the universe. He needs no one's opinion or assistance. He makes decisions for all of mankind because his ways are higher than our ways and his thoughts far above our thoughts. He does whatever he desires, and it is according to his perfectly planned will. And when he does move, his actions are gratifying to him. We were created for his pleasure, and he leads us down paths for our good because of his great love for us.

What are you still holding on to that you need to give up control over?

Stable

"I have told you all this so that you may have peace in me. Here on earth you will have many trials and sorrows. But take heart, because I have overcome the world."

JOHN 16:33 NLT

The woman told her daughter to take a deep breath. She stroked her hair and held her close as the child's tears fell. She had been out riding her bike with friends and took a nasty fall, leaving her with a deep gash. As the doctor sewed up the wound, he tried to remind her that someday, this would be a dim memory, and the scar would fade. For now, he advised her, it would be best to remain as still and calm as possible.

Jesus didn't want us to be blindsided about what we would encounter here on earth. He knew that living in this world would come with great troubles. He knew we had an enemy that was out for our blood. At times, we fall prey to heart sickness, and worry fills our souls. He was straight with us about what we would face, but he also told us the end game. We win because of his victory on the cross. We can rest through hardships in faith because he has overcome through us and for us.

When trials appear, how can you trust Jesus as your stability?

Ambitious

We make it our goal to please him,
whether we are at home in the body or away from it.
2 CORINTHIANS 5:9 NIV

She couldn't figure out what she had done wrong. She kept with the program, enhanced it with her ideas, put in weeks of work, and it still seemed like she couldn't please everyone. She had known her efforts would be scrutinized, but she'd felt like she was up to the challenge. Now, she was being told that all of it would have to be redone and that they would be replacing her. She left bewildered and determined not to seek any other person's approval again.

When we make it our mission to please Jesus, we will never be told that our goal is not good enough or that our personal offering has missed the mark. We're not required to do any kind of work for our salvation. It is God's gift. We are not to strive or trust in our own ability, for apart from Christ, we can do nothing. As Christians, we are accepted as beloved. Period. Case closed. As his own, he will never turn us away. As we come to him, he will welcome his children with approval and open arms.

When you stand before Jesus, will your life have been lived for him?

Calm

Cast all your anxiety on him because he cares for you.

1 PETER 5:7 NRSV

Have you ever been told not to worry? To just relax and let everything work out? Sounds easy, and over-simplified, doesn't it? How many people in our society find themselves stressed, obsessed with what the future might or might not hold? In the world, there are few strategies for solving the ills of anxiety other than medical means. There are classes on calming yourself and apps to help you shut off your mind and go to sleep, but as soon as a crisis arrives, those aids lose their power.

God never intended for us to suffer from anguish over uncertainty. From the beginning, he designed us to depend on him for everything, including our next breath. When we're caught up in concern, we're really telling the Father that we don't trust him to handle it. He has proven his faithfulness, and he has given us a way to squash worry—prayer. We can ask him to take the reins, provide what we need, and thank him for his constant protection, provision, and for answering our prayers. Be still. Let him control the outcome.

How can you choose not to worry and rest in the fact that your heavenly Father knows best?

Meek

*"I am the light of the world.
Whoever follows me will not walk in darkness
but will have the light of life."*

JOHN 8:12 ESV

The men were exhausted from working a long day of guiding their sheep through hills and valleys. They had settled in a field for the night, allowing the animals to rest under their watchful eye and diligent care. It was just another evening in the life of a shepherd. They would never have imagined they were about to hear the heavenly host singing, "Glory to God in the highest, and on earth peace among men!" This would come on the heels of a fearful moment where an angel abruptly appeared in their midst, announcing that the long-awaited Messiah had been born.

"What palace is he in?" they might have asked. There was no glorious arrival into his earthly kingdom; he came in humility, in the form of a human infant, the Savior of the world. The star in the sky that night led the way to the light of the world. No more would humanity need to live in darkness, for Jesus came to defeat sin and death and offer salvation to all.

This Christmas Eve, will you reflect on the fact that God became man to save you?

Wonderful

Unto us a Child is born, unto us a Son is given; and the government will be upon His shoulder. And His name will be called Wonderful, Counselor, Mighty God, Everlasting Father, Prince of Peace.

ISAIAH 9:6 NKJV

"Happy Birthday, Jesus!" the family exclaimed. They all put aside the materialism of Christmas, placing all their focus on the birth of their Savior. They still had a tree and a few presents, but they decided not to follow the world or the commercialization of the day. There was no hustle and bustle, but there was a birthday cake, songs of praise, and the presence of the Savior as they honored his coming to earth for mankind.

How many of us place more importance on the fact that unto us a child was given, rather than making sure we got gifts for everyone who might get us one? It is easy to get absorbed in the demands of the holiday, but we can control how we acknowledge it. As you celebrate the birth of Christ today, remember that we have been given the greatest gift of all—our wonderful Savior. Recall his names as you prepare your heart for the festivities. He is Wonderful, Counselor, Mighty God, Everlasting Father, and Prince of Peace. We are his, and he is ours.

Will you start a new tradition by centering your Christmas activities around Jesus?

Breathtaking

The LORD your God is God of gods and LORD of lords, the great, the mighty, and the awesome God, who is not partial and takes no bribe.

DEUTERONOMY 10:17 ESV

The pastor decided to give his church a little object lesson. He hired an actor to dress as a homeless person and sleep on the church steps until the morning service. The actor made sure that he had not showered, that his clothes were dirty and his hair disheveled. When the congregation was seated, he walked down the aisle in full view and sat in the front. The pastor watched his flock to see if they welcomed him or shied away from him.

As soon as the service ended, two men made a beeline for the homeless man, welcoming him, offering him lunch, and seeing what they could do to alter his situation. No one looked down on him; they only asked how they could lift him up. The pastor watched with tear-filled eyes. His followers had not only been listening to his lessons, but they were also putting them into practice. In the same way, God accepts all his creation, and he doesn't play favorites. His goodness and love are never limited to certain individuals but are available to all. Shouldn't we do the same?

Do you accept all who are made in God's image?

Chosen

*"You did not choose Me but I chose you,
and appointed you that you would go and bear fruit,
and that your fruit would remain."*

JOHN 15:16 NASB

The college decided to choose one female to represent their student body as the ideal of what they desired their undergraduates to aspire to be. This individual would have an exceptional grade point average, be involved in campus clubs, and seek to show kindness to everyone, lending a helping hand to all. This desired award would look great on a grad school application, and it inspired many of the college's young women into action in hopes that they would be chosen.

When we understand that we had nothing to do with the fact that we are chosen by God, we are humbled and grateful. He is the one who selected us. He loved us first, not the other way around. When we were rebellious in nature, he also chose to come to earth and take our place on the cross for our sins. He has given us everything in Christ. As his image bearers, we are called to the great commission. It is his will that we go into all the world in his name, taking the gospel to as many as possible and making disciples for Jesus.

When God calls you, will you readily say, "Here I am, send me"?

Exalted

*"All who exalt themselves will be humbled,
and all who humble themselves will be exalted."*
MATTHEW 23:12 NRSV

The outside hitter on the volleyball team was racking up points in the tournament. Her teammates were giving her high fives every chance they got and shouting accolades. When the exceptional player made the winning point, they gathered her on their shoulders and carried her off the court. The girls started to regret the attention they gave her when she started to sing her own praises in excess. When the next game came, she'd gotten a bit too big for her britches, and now overconfident, she missed almost all her hits.

In his kindness, God warns us what will happen when we think too highly of ourselves. Pride is eventually followed by a fall. The Lord is the only one who exalts his children. If we attempt to place ourselves on a pedestal, he will see to it, for our own well-being, that the bottom falls out. Our Father detests it when our ego gets inflated. In fact, the Bible says it is an abomination to him. If you desire to live in God's continued grace, make certain your heart is not prideful.

How can you boast in the Lord instead of in yourself?

Fascinating

Many, LORD my God, are the wonders
which You have done,
And Your thoughts toward us;
There is none to compare with You.
If I would declare and speak of them,
They would be too numerous to count.

PSALM 40:5 NASB

If you go to a small county fair, you might see an exhibit that says, "See the Seven Wonders of the World!" The exhibit would contain small replicas of the original seven wonders or perhaps the new seven wonders. If you were able to leave that event and travel the globe, you could visit the actual treasures. From the symbol of the Inca civilization, Machu Picchu in Peru, to Christ the Redeemer statue in Brazil, and on to the Great Wall of China, you would witness thrilling monuments.

Nothing, though, can compare to the magnificence of creation or the supernatural acts of our God. If we had seen the parting of the Red Sea, the flood in Noah's day, or observed Jesus walking the land after his resurrection, we would have viewed the truth of real miracles with our own eyes. Nothing man could ever think or create can come close to God's revelations and masterpieces. The multitude of his works declare his glory, and in every instance, he did it with us in mind.

When you consider that God had you in mind before and during his creation, how does that make you feel?

Exemplary

"Let your light shine before others, that they may see your good deeds and glorify your Father in heaven."
MATTHEW 5:16 NIV

She was known as the neighborhood's angel. Any time a new family moved in on her street, she was there with a welcome basket. If a resident were ill, she'd cook up a batch of chicken soup and make sure that person had groceries delivered if needed. When an elderly couple needed a ride or an errand done, she was the first to offer assistance. Everyone wondered what compelled her. When they asked, she was ready with her answer.

The woman above was doing exactly what Scripture instructs us to do. We are to put the concerns of others first. Our eyes and ears should be attentive to those around us and how we can step in and help in their time of need. Even a simple plate of cookies can brighten someone's day. When the woman was asked why she was so kind and giving to others, she said, "It is because of what Jesus has given me." Her good deeds gave her the chance to shine her light and spread the good news, which brought God's favor and gave him glory.

Is your heart light shining bright, or is its wattage low?

Consecrated

*I appeal to you therefore, brothers, by the mercies of
God, to present your bodies as a living sacrifice, holy and
acceptable to God, which is your spiritual worship.*

ROMANS 12:1 ESV

Once the young man willingly signed the papers, he was a
member of the U.S. military. For the next few years, they would
not ask what he wanted. They, for all intents and purposes,
would have control over his coming and going. He would join a
squadron, doing battle and giving aid in the country where he
was stationed, obeying every order so he stayed in good graces
with his superior officers. He would give his best to support his
fellow soldiers and serve his country.

As Christians, we are to sacrifice our entire beings to God for
his service. He will never make us comply; he gently requests
that we offer ourselves up. It is entirely up to us whether we
want to surrender and place ourselves on his altar so he can
be triumphant through us. Jesus Christ bought us with the
price of his broken body and shed blood, making us holy and
acceptable to the Father. When we fully commit our hearts,
minds, souls, and bodies to his good and perfect will, we are
offering him the best of our spiritual worship.

*Do you own your life, or does God? How can you consecrate the
new year to him?*

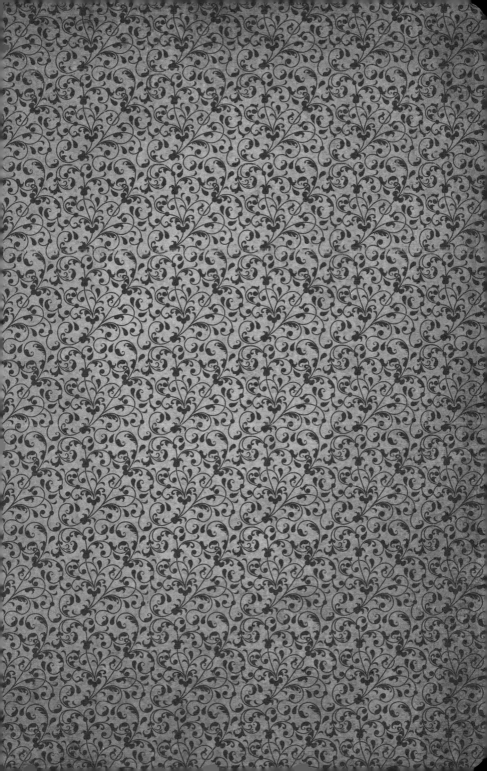